SOURCE
The Prentice Hall
ENGINEERING SOURCE

Power Programming
with VBA/Excel®

Steven C. Chapra

Tufts University

Pearson Education, Inc.
Upper Saddle River, NJ 07458

Library of Congress Cataloging-in-Publication Data Available

Vice President and Editorial Director, ECS: *Marcia J.Horton*
Executive Editor: *Eric Svendsen*
Associate Editor: *Dee Bernhard*
Vice President and Director of Production and Manufacturing, ESM: *David W. Riccardi*
Executive Managing Editor: *Vince O'Brien*
Managing Editor: *David A. George*
Production Editor: *Rose Kernan*
Director of Creative Services: *Paul Belfanti*
Creative Director: *Carole Anson*
Art Director: *Jayne Conte*
Art Editor: *Greg Dulles*
Manufacturing Manager: *Trudy Pisciotti*
Manufacturing Buyer: *Lisa McDowell*
Marketing Manager: *Holly Stark*

© 2003 Pearson Education, Inc.
Upper Saddle River, New Jersey 07458

The author and publisher of this book have used their best efforts in preparing this book. These efforts include the development, research, and testing of the theories and programs to determine their effectiveness. The author and publisher shall not be liable in any event for incidental or consequential damages in connection with, or arising out of, the furnishing, performance, or use of these programs.

Visual Basic and Excel are registered trademarks of the Microsoft Corporation, One Microsoft Way, Redmond, WA 98052-6399

Printed in the United States of America.

10 9 8 7 6 5 4 3 2 1

ISBN 0-13-047377-4

Pearson Education Ltd., *London*
Pearson Education Australia Pty. Ltd., *Sydney*
Pearson Education Singapore, Pte. Ltd.
Pearson Education North Asia Ltd., *Hong Kong*
Pearson Education Canada, Inc., *Toronto*
Pearson Educacíon de Mexico, S.A. de C.V.
Pearson Education—Japan, *Tokyo*
Pearson Education Malaysia, Pte. Ltd.
Pearson Education, *Upper Saddle River, New Jersey*

About ESource

ESource—The Prentice Hall Engineering Source—
www.prenhall.com/esource

ESource—The Prentice Hall Engineering Source gives professors the power to harness the full potential of their text and their first-year engineering course. More than just a collection of books, ESource is a unique publishing system revolving around the ESource website—www.prenhall.com/esource. ESource enables you to put your stamp on your book just as you do your course. It lets you:

Control   You choose exactly what chapter or sections are in your book and in what order they appear. Of course, you can choose the entire book if you'd like and stay with the authors' original order.

Optimize   Get the most from your book and your course. ESource lets you produce the optimal text for your students needs.

Customize   You can add your own material anywhere in your text's presentation, and your final product will arrive at your bookstore as a professionally formatted text. Of course, all titles in this series are available as stand-alone texts, or as bundles of two or more books sold at a discount. Contact your PH sales rep for discount information.

ESource ACCESS

Professors who choose to bundle two or more texts from the ESource series for their class, or use an ESource custom book will be providing their students with complete access to the library of ESource content. All bundles and custom books will come with a student password that gives web ESource ACCESS to all information on the site. This passcode is free and is valid for one year after initial log-on. We've designed ESource ACCESS to provide students a flexible, searchable, on-line resource. Professors may also choose to deliver custom ESource content via the web only using ESource ACCESS passcodes. Contact your PH sales rep for more information.

ESource Content

All the content in ESource was written by educators specifically for freshman/first-year students. Authors tried to strike a balanced level of presentation, an approach that was neither formulaic nor trivial, and one that did not focus too heavily on advanced topics that most introductory students do not encounter until later classes. Because many professors do not have extensive time to cover these topics in the classroom, authors prepared each text with the idea that many students would use it for self-instruction and independent study. Students should be able to use this content to learn the software tool or subject on their own.

While authors had the freedom to write texts in a style appropriate to their particular subject, all followed certain guidelines created to promote a consistency that makes students comfortable. Namely, every chapter opens with a clear set of **Objectives**, includes **Practice Boxes** throughout the chapter, and ends with a number of **Problems**, and a list of **Key Terms**. **Applications Boxes** are spread throughout the book with the intent of giving students a real-world perspective of engineering. **Success Boxes** provide the student with advice about college study skills, and help students avoid the common pitfalls of first-year students. In addition, this series contains an entire book titled **Engineering Success** by Peter Schiavone of the University of Alberta intended to expose students quickly to what it takes to be an engineering student.

Creating Your Book

Using ESource is simple. You preview the content either on-line or through examination copies of the books you can request on-line, from your PH sales rep, or by calling 1-800-526-0485. Create an on-line outline of the content you want, in the order you want, using ESource's simple interface. Either type or cut and paste your own material and insert it into the text flow. You can preview the overall organization of the text you've created at anytime (please note, since this preview is immediate, it comes unformatted.), then press another button and receive an order number for your own custom book. If you are not ready to order, do nothing—ESource will save your work. You can come back at any time and change, re-arrange, or add more material to your creation. Once you're finished and you have an ISBN, give it to your bookstore and your book will arrive on their shelves four to six weeks after they order. Your custom desk copies with their instructor supplements will arrive at your address at the same time.

To learn more about this new system for creating the perfect textbook, go to www.prenhall.com/esource. You can either go through the on-line walkthrough of how to create a book, or experiment yourself.

Supplements

Adopters of ESource receive an instructor's CD that contains professor and student code from the books in the series, as well as other instruction aides provided by authors. The website also holds approximately **350 PowerPoint transparencies** created by Jack Leifer of University of Kentucky–Paducah available to download. Professors can either follow these transparencies as pre-prepared lectures or use them as the basis for their own custom presentations.

Titles in the ESource Series

Design Concepts for Engineers, 2/e
0-13-093430-5
Mark Horenstein

Engineering Success, 2/e
0-13-041827-7
Peter Schiavone

Engineering Design and Problem Solving, 2E
ISBN 0-13-093399-6
Steven K. Howell

Exploring Engineering
ISBN 0-13-093442-9
Joe King

Engineering Ethics
0-13-784224-4
Charles B. Fleddermann

Engineering Design—A Day in the Life of Four Engineers
0-13-085089-6
Mark N. Horenstein

Introduction to Engineering Analysis
0-13-016733-9
Kirk D. Hagen

Introduction to Engineering Experimentation
0-13-032835-9
Ronald W. Larsen, John T. Sears, and Royce Wilkinson

Introduction to Mechanical Engineering
0-13-019640-1
Robert Rizza

Introduction to Electrical and Computer Engineering
0-13-033363-8
Charles B. Fleddermann and Martin Bradshaw

Introduction to MATLAB 6
0-13-032845-6
Delores Etter and David C. Kuncicky, with Douglas W. Hull

Introduction to MATLAB
0-13-013149-0
Delores Etter with David C. Kuncicky

Introduction to Mathcad 2000
0-13-020007-7
Ronald W. Larsen

Introduction to Mathcad
0-13-937493-0
Ronald W. Larsen

Introduction to Maple
0-13-095133-1
David I. Schwartz

Mathematics Review
0-13-011501-0
Peter Schiavone

Power Programming with VBA/Excel
0-13-047377-4
Steven C. Chapra

Introduction to Excel 2002
0-13-008175-2
David C. Kuncicky

About the Authors

Stephen J. Chapman received a B.S. degree in Electrical Engineering from Louisiana State University (1975), the M.S.E. degree in Electrical Engineering from the University of Central Florida (1979), and pursued further graduate studies at Rice University.

Mr. Chapman is currently Manager of Technical Systems for British Aerospace Australia, in Melbourne, Australia. In this position, he provides technical direction and design authority for the work of younger engineers within the company. He also continues to teach at local universities on a part-time basis.

Mr. Chapman is a Senior Member of the Institute of Electrical and Electronics Engineers (and several of its component societies). He is also a member of the Association for Computing Machinery and the Institution of Engineers (Australia).

N o project could ever come to pass without a group of authors who have the vision and the courage to turn a stack of blank paper into a book. The authors in this series, who worked diligently to produce their books, provide the building blocks of the series.

Martin D. Bradshaw was born in Pittsburg, KS in 1936, grew up in Kansas and the surrounding states of Arkansas and Missouri, graduating from Newton High School, Newton, KS in 1954. He received the B.S.E.E. and M.S.E. degrees from the University of Wichita in 1958 and 1961, respectively. A Ford Foundation fellowship at Carnegie Institute of Technology followed from 1961 to 1963 and he received the Ph.D. degree in electrical engineering in 1964. He spent his entire academic career with the Department of Electrical and Computer Engineering at the University of New Mexico (1961-1963 and 1991-1996). He served as the Assistant Dean for Special Programs with the UNM College of Engineering from 1974 to 1976 and as the Associate Chairman for the EECE Department from 1993 to 1996. During the period 1987-1991 he was a consultant with his own company, EE Problem Solvers. During 1978 he spent a sabbatical year with the State Electricity Commission of Victoria, Melbourne, Australia. From 1979 to 1981 he served an IPA assignment as a Project Officer at the U.S. Air Force Weapons Laboratory, Kirkland AFB, Albuquerque, NM. He has won numerous local, regional, and national teaching awards, including the George Westinghouse Award from the ASEE in 1973. He was awarded the IEEE Centennial Medal in 2000.

Acknowledgments: Dr. Bradshaw would like to acknowledge his late mother, who gave him a great love of reading and learning, and his father, who taught him to persist until the job is finished. The encouragement of his wife, Jo, and his six children is a never-ending inspiration.

Steven C. Chapra presently holds the Louis Berger Chair for Computing and Engineering in the Civil and Environmental Engineering Department at Tufts University. Dr. Chapra received engineering degrees from Manhattan College and the University of Michigan. Before joining the faculty at Tufts, he taught at Texas A&M University, the University of Colorado, and Imperial College, London. His research interests focus on surface water-quality modeling and advanced computer applications in environmental engineering. He has published over 50 refereed journal articles, 20 software packages and 6 books. He has received a number of awards including the 1987 ASEE Merriam/Wiley Distinguished Author Award, the 1993 Rudolph Hering Medal, and teaching awards from Texas A&M, the University of Colorado, and the Association of Environmental Engineering and Science Professors.

Acknowledgments: To the Berger Family for their many contributions to engineering education. I would also like to thank David Clough for his friendship and insights, John Walkenbach for his wonderful books, and my colleague Lee Minardi and my students Kenny William, Robert Viesca and Jennifer Edelmann for their suggestions.

Mark Dix began working with AutoCAD in 1985 as a programmer for CAD Support Associates, Inc. He helped design a system for creating estimates and bills of material directly from AutoCAD drawing databases for use in the automated conveyor industry. This system became the basis for systems still widely in use today. In 1986 he began collaborating with Paul Riley to create AutoCAD training materials, combining Riley's background in industrial design and training with Dix's background in writing, curriculum development, and programming. Mr. Dix received the M.S. degree in education from the University of Massachusetts. He is currently the Director of Dearborn Academy High School in Arlington, Massachusetts.

Delores M. Etter is a Professor of Electrical and Computer Engineering at the University of Colorado. Dr. Etter was a faculty member at the University of New Mexico and also a Visiting Professor at Stanford University. Dr. Etter was responsible for the Freshman Engineering Program at the University of New Mexico and is active in the Integrated Teaching Laboratory at the University of Colorado. She was elected a Fellow of the Institute of Electrical and Electronics Engineers for her contributions to education and for her technical leadership in digital signal processing.

Charles B. Fleddermann is a professor in the Department of Electrical and Computer Engineering at the University of New Mexico in Albuquerque, New Mexico. All of his degrees are in electrical engineering: his Bachelor's degree from the University of Notre Dame, and the Master's and Ph.D. from the University of Illinois at Urbana-Champaign. Prof. Fleddermann developed an engineering ethics course for his department in response to the ABET requirement to incorporate ethics topics into the undergraduate engineering curriculum. *Engineering Ethics* was written as a vehicle for presenting ethical theory, analysis, and problem solving to engineering undergraduates in a concise and readily accessible way.

Acknowledgments: I would like to thank Profs. Charles Harris and Michael Rabins of Texas A & M University whose NSF sponsored workshops on engineering ethics got me started thinking in this field. Special thanks to my wife Liz, who proofread the manuscript for this book, provided many useful suggestions, and who helped me learn how to teach "soft" topics to engineers.

Kirk D. Hagen is a professor at Weber State University in Ogden, Utah. He has taught introductory-level engineering courses and upper-division thermal science courses at WSU since 1993. He received his B.S. degree in physics from Weber State College and his M.S. degree in mechanical engineering from Utah State University, after which he worked as a thermal designer/analyst in the aerospace and electronics industries. After several years of engineering practice, he resumed his formal education, earning his Ph.D. in mechanical engineering at the University of Utah. Hagen is the author of an undergraduate heat transfer text.

Mark N. Horenstein is a Professor in the Department of Electrical and Computer Engineering at Boston University. He has degrees in Electrical Engineering from M.I.T. and U.C. Berkeley and has been involved in teaching engineering design for the greater part of his academic career. He devised and developed the senior design project class taken by all electrical and computer engineering students at Boston University. In this class, the students work for a virtual engineering company developing products and systems for real-world engineering and social-service clients.

Acknowledgments: I would like to thank Prof. James Bethune, the architect of the Peak Performance event at Boston University, for his permission to highlight the competition in my text. Several of the ideas relating to brainstorming and teamwork were derived from a workshop on engineering design offered by Prof. Charles Lovas of Southern Methodist University. The principles of estimation were derived in part from a freshman engineering problem posed by Prof. Thomas Kincaid of Boston University.

Steven Howell is the Chairman and a Professor of Mechanical Engineering at Lawrence Technological University. Prior to joining LTU in 2001, Dr. Howell led a knowledge-based engineering project for Visteon Automotive Systems and taught computer-aided design  classes for Ford Motor Company engineers. Dr. Howell also has a total of 15 years experience as an engineering faculty member at Northern Arizona University, the University of the Pacific, and the University of Zimbabwe. While at Northern Arizona University, he helped develop and implement an award-winning interdisciplinary series of design courses simulating a corporate engineering-design environment.

Douglas W. Hull is a graduate student in the Department of Mechanical Engineering at Carnegie Mellon University in Pittsburgh, Pennsylvania. He is the author of *Mastering Mechanics I Using Matlab 5*, and contributed to *Mechanics of Materials* by Bedford and Liechti. His  research in the Sensor Based Planning lab involves motion planning for hyper-redundant manipulators, also known as serpentine robots.

Scott D. James is a staff lecturer at Kettering University (formerly GMI Engineering & Management Institute) in Flint, Michigan. He is currently pursuing a Ph.D. in Systems Engineering with an emphasis on software engineering and computer-integrated manufac-  turing. He chose teaching as a profession after several years in the computer industry. "I thought that it was really important to know what it was like outside of academia. I wanted to provide students with classes that were up to date and provide the information that is really used and needed."

Acknowledgments: Scott would like to acknowledge his family for the time to work on the text and his students and peers at Kettering who offered helpful critiques of the materials that eventually became the book.

Joe King received the B.S. and M.S. degrees from the University of California at Davis. He is a Professor of Computer Engineering at the University of the Pacific, Stockton, CA, where he teaches courses in digital design, computer design, artificial intelligence, and com-  puter networking. Since joining the UOP faculty, Professor King has spent yearlong sabbaticals teaching in Zimbabwe, Singapore, and Finland. A licensed engineer in the state of California, King's industrial experience includes major design projects with Lawrence Livermore National Laboratory, as well as independent consulting projects. Prof. King has had a number of books published with titles including MATLAB, MathCAD, Exploring Engineering, and Engineering and Society.

David C. Kuncicky is a native Floridian. He earned his Baccalaureate in psychology, Master's in computer science, and Ph.D. in computer science from Florida State University. He has served as a faculty member in the Department of Electrical Engineering at the FAMU–  FSU College of Engineering and the Department of Computer Science at Florida State University. He has taught computer science and computer engineering courses for over 15 years. He has published research in the areas of intelligent hybrid systems and neural networks. He is currently the Director of Engineering at Bioreason, Inc. in Sante Fe, New Mexico.

Acknowledgments: Thanks to Steffie and Helen for putting up with my late nights and long weekends at the computer. Finally, thanks to Susan Bassett for having faith in my abilities, and for providing continued tutelage and support.

Ron Larsen is a Professor of Chemical Engineering at Montana State University, and received his Ph.D. from the Pennsylvania State University. He was initially attracted to engineering by the challenges the profession offers, but also appreciates that engineering is a serving profession. Some of the greatest challenges he has faced while teaching have involved non-traditional teaching methods, including evening courses for practicing engineers and teaching through an interpreter at the Mongolian National University. These experiences have provided tremendous opportunities to learn new ways to communicate technical material. Dr. Larsen views modern software as one of the new tools that will radically alter the way engineers work, and his book *Introduction to Math-CAD* was written to help young engineers prepare to meet the challenges of an ever-changing workplace.

Acknowledgments: To my students at Montana State University who have endured the rough drafts and typos, and who still allow me to experiment with their classes— my sincere thanks.

Sanford Leestma is a Professor of Mathematics and Computer Science at Calvin College, and received his Ph.D. from New Mexico State University. He has been the long-time co-author of successful textbooks on Fortran, Pascal, and data structures in Pascal. His current research interest are in the areas of algorithms and numerical computation.

Jack Leifer is an Assistant Professor in the Department of Mechanical Engineering at the University of Kentucky Extended Campus Program in Paducah, and was previously with the Department of Mathematical Sciences and Engineering at the University of South Carolina–Aiken. He received his Ph.D. in Mechanical Engineering from the University of Texas at Austin in December 1995. His current research interests include the modeling of sensors for manufacturing, and the use of Artificial Neural Networks to predict corrosion.

Acknowledgments: I'd like to thank my colleagues at USC–Aiken, especially Professors Mike May and Laurene Fausett, for their encouragement and feedback; and my parents, Felice and Morton Leifer, for being there and providing support (as always) as I completed this book.

Richard M. Lueptow is the Charles Deering McCormick Professor of Teaching Excellence and Associate Professor of Mechanical Engineering at Northwestern University. He is a native of Wisconsin and received his doctorate from the Massachusetts Institute of Technology in 1986. He teaches design, fluid mechanics, an spectral analysis techniques. Rich has an active research program on rotating filtration, Taylor Couette flow, granular flow, fire suppression, and acoustics. He has five patents and over 40 refereed journal and proceedings papers along with many other articles, abstracts, and presentations.

Acknowledgments: Thanks to my talented and hard-working co-authors as well as the many colleagues and students who took the tutorial for a "test drive." Special thanks to Mike Minbiole for his major contributions to Graphics Concepts with SolidWorks. Thanks also to Northwestern University for the time to work on a book. Most of all, thanks to my loving wife, Maiya, and my children, Hannah and Kyle, for supporting me in this endeavor. (Photo courtesy of Evanston Photographic Studios, Inc.)

Larry Nyhoff is a Professor of Mathematics and Computer Science at Calvin College. After doing bachelor's work at Calvin, and Master's work at Michigan, he received a Ph.D. from Michigan State and also did graduate work in computer science at Western Michigan. Dr. Nyhoff has taught at Calvin for the past 34 years—mathematics at first and computer science for the past several years.

Acknowledgments: We thank our families—Shar, Jeff, Dawn, Rebecca, Megan, Sara, Greg, Julie, Joshua, Derek, Tom, Joan; Marge, Michelle, Sandy, Lory, Michael—for being patient and understanding. We thank God for allowing us to write this text.

Paul Riley is an author, instructor, and designer specializing in graphics and design for multimedia. He is a founding partner of CAD Support Associates, a contract service and professional training organization for computer-aided design. His 15 years of business experience and 20 years of teaching experience are supported by degrees in education and computer science. Paul has taught AutoCAD at the University of Massachusetts at Lowell and is presently teaching AutoCAD at Mt. Ida College in Newton, Massachusetts. He has developed a program,

Computer-aided Design for Professionals that is highly regarded by corporate clients and has been an ongoing success since 1982.

Robert Rizza is an Assistant Professor of Mechanical Engineering at North Dakota State University, where he teaches courses in mechanics and computer-aided design. A native of Chicago, he received the Ph.D. degree from the Illinois Institute of Technology. He is also the author of *Getting Started with Pro/ENGINEER*.  Dr. Rizza has worked on a diverse range of engineering projects including projects from the railroad, bioengineering, and aerospace industries. His current research interests include the fracture of composite materials, repair of cracked aircraft components, and loosening of prostheses.

Peter Schiavone is a professor and student advisor in the Department of Mechanical Engineering at the University of Alberta, Canada. He received his Ph.D. from the University of Strathclyde, U.K. in 1988. He has authored several books in the area of student academic success as well as numerous papers in international scientific research journals. Dr. Schiavone has worked in private industry in several different areas of engineering including aerospace and systems engineering. He founded the first Mathematics Resource Center at the University of Alberta, a unit designed specifically  to teach new students the necessary *survival skills* in mathematics and the physical sciences required for success in first-year engineering. This led to the Students' Union Gold Key Award for outstanding contributions to the university. Dr. Schiavone lectures regularly to freshman engineering students and to new engineering professors on engineering success, in particular about maximizing students' academic performance.

Acknowledgements: Thanks to Richard Felder for being such an inspiration; to my wife Linda for sharing my dreams and believing in me; and to Francesca and Antonio for putting up with Dad when working on the text.

David I. Schneider holds an A.B. degree from Oberlin College and a Ph.D. degree in Mathematics from MIT. He has taught for 34 years, primarily at the University of Maryland. Dr. Schneider has authored 28 books, with one-half of them computer programming books. He has developed three customized  software packages that are supplied as supplements to over 55 mathematics textbooks. His involvement with computers dates back to 1962, when he programmed a special purpose computer at MIT's Lincoln Laboratory to correct errors in a communications system.

David I. Schwartz is an Assistant Professor in the Computer Science Department at Cornell University and earned his B.S., M.S., and Ph.D. degrees in Civil Engineering from State University of New York at Buffalo. Throughout his graduate studies, Schwartz combined  principles of computer science to applications of civil engineering. He became interested in helping students learn how to apply software tools for solving a variety of engineering problems. He teaches his students to learn incrementally and practice frequently to gain the maturity to tackle other subjects. In his spare time, Schwartz plays drums in a variety of bands.

Acknowledgments: I dedicate my books to my family, friends, and students who all helped in so many ways.

Many thanks go to the schools of Civil Engineering and Engineering & Applied Science at State University of New York at Buffalo where I originally developed and tested my UNIX and Maple books. I greatly appreciate the opportunity to explore my goals and all the help from everyone at the Computer Science Department at Cornell.

 **John T. Sears** received the Ph.D. degree from Princeton University. Currently, he is a Professor and the head of the Department of Chemical Engineering at Montana State University. After leaving Princeton he worked in research at Brookhaven National Laboratory and Esso Research and Engineering, until he took a position at West Virginia University. He came to MSU in 1982, where he has served as the Director of the College of Engineering Minority Program and Interim Director for BioFilm Engineering. Prof. Sears has written a book on air pollution and economic development, and over 45 articles in engineering and engineering education.

 **Michael T. Snyder** is President of Internet startup Appointments123.com. He is a native of Chicago, and he received his Bachelor of Science degree in Mechanical Engineering from the University of Notre Dame. Mike also graduated with honors from Northwestern University's Kellogg Graduate School of Management in 1999 with his Masters of Management degree. Before Appointments123.com, Mike was a mechanical engineer in new product development for Motorola Cellular and Acco Office Products. He has received four patents for his mechanical design work. "Pro/ENGINEER was an invaluable design tool for me,

and I am glad to help students learn the basics of Pro/ENGINEER."

Acknowledgments: Thanks to Rich Lueptow and Jim Steger for inviting me to be a part of this great project. Of course, thanks to my wife Gretchen for her support in my various projects.

 **Jim Steger** is currently Chief Technical Officer and cofounder of an Internet applications company. He graduated with a Bachelor of Science degree in Mechanical Engineering from Northwestern University. His prior work included mechanical engineering assignments at Motorola and Acco Brands. At Motorola, Jim worked on part design for two-way radios and was one of the lead mechanical engineers on a cellular phone product line. At Acco Brands, Jim was the sole engineer on numerous office product designs. His Worx stapler has won design awards in the United States and in Europe. Jim has been a Pro/ENGINEER user for over six years.

Acknowledgments: Many thanks to my co-authors, especially Rich Lueptow for his leadership on this project. I would also like to thank my family for their continuous support.

 **Royce Wilkinson** received his undergraduate degree in chemistry from Rose-Hulman Institute of Technology in 1991 and the Ph.D. degree in chemistry from Montana State University in 1998 with research in natural product isolation from fungi. He currently resides in Bozeman, MT and is involved in HIV drug research. His research interests center on biological molecules and their interactions in the search for pharmaceutical advances.

Contents

1

If You've Never Programmed Before

Although some readers will have some previous programming experience, this may be your first exposure to programming. Therefore, I've written this chapter to provide some fundamental prerequisite concepts for those who have never programmed before. In particular, it is critical that neophytes understand the following three topics:

- Programs
- Assignment
- Decisions and Loops

If you are a veteran programmer, most of this chapter will be rudimentary. However, for those programmers who are unfamiliar with Basic, you should read the last two sections. These are designed to acquaint you with how VBA represents decisions (that is, If statements) and count-controlled loops.

OBJECTIVES

After reading this chapter, you should be able to

- Understand the "idea" of a program.
- Understand the concept of "assignment."
- Write simple decisions and loops.

1.1 THE "IDEA" OF A PROGRAM

Computer programs are like road directions. Suppose I want to tell someone how to drive from point *A* to point *B*. Here's an example:

1. Leave parking lot and turn right onto Winter Street
2. Drive 1 mile
3. Turn right onto Route 30 East
4. Drive 0.5 mile
5. Turn left onto Wellesley Street
6. Drive 0.8 mile
7. Turn left onto Chestnut Street.

A person could follow these directions in a step-by-step fashion and arrive at Chestnut Street with no problem.

However, suppose that we switched two of the instructions:

1. Leave parking lot and turn right onto Winter Street
2. Drive 1 mile
3. Turn left onto Wellesley Street
4. Drive 0.5 mile
5. Turn right onto Route 30 East
6. Drive 0.8 mile
7. Turn left onto Chestnut Street.

As a consequence, the individual would become hopelessly lost. To be effective, road directions must be unambiguous and totally logical. If not, they won't work the way you want them to.

The same holds true for computer programs. A *program* is a sequence of unambiguous instructions that the computer implements one after another in a mindless fashion. These instructions are sometimes called *statements*. For example, a very simple VBA Sub program to add two numbers can be written as

```
Sub Adder()
a = 10
b = 33
c = a + b
End Sub
```

It's not too difficult to see that this program assigns two numeric constants to the variables a and b, and then adds them and assigns the result to the variable c.

Now, suppose you redid the program and switched two of the statements:

```
Sub Adder()
a = 10
c = a + b
b = 33
End Sub
```

This wouldn't give the desired result, because the program performs the addition prior to assigning a value to b. Therefore, c would have a value of 10, rather than the desired result: 43.

Although this example is trivial, it serves to make an important point that novice programmers must understand: The computer is like an *idiot savant* who can implement instructions at an incredibly fast rate. However, if your instructions to it (i.e., the program) are ambiguous and illogical, it just won't work properly.

1.2 THE CONCEPT OF ASSIGNMENT

In the previous section, we used terms like "constants," "variables," and "assignment." Let's now make certain that you understand what these terms and their ramifications for computer equations mean.

There are two fundamental ways in which information is represented in a computer language like VBA: directly as constants and symbolically as variables. As the name implies, a *constant* is a value that does not change. In contrast, a *variable* is a symbolic name that can take on different values. They are related by the fact that constants can be assigned to variables, as in Figure 1.1.

It is useful to understand what the computer actually does when an assignment statement is executed. The variable is the label that the computer associates with the memory location where it stores a constant value. As depicted in Figure 1.2, the first two statements,

```
a = 10
b = 33
```

cause the computer to set up two storage locations in its memory which it labels as a and b, and into which it stores the constants 10 and 33. The third statement,

```
c = a + b
```

instructs the computer to add the stored values of the variables a and b, and to assign the result to the variable c.

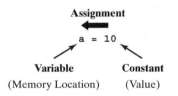

Figure 1.1.   A VBA assignment statement in which constants is assigned to a variable.

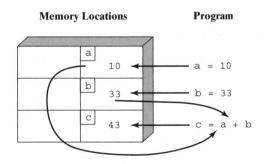

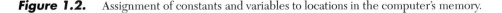

Figure 1.2.   Assignment of constants and variables to locations in the computer's memory.

The equals sign in the assignment statement can be thought of as meaning "is replaced by" or "is assigned the result." It is critical to recognize that this use is different from the conventional one wherein the equals sign signifies equality. The distinction is so significant that some computer scientists have actually suggested that a better representation would be an arrow:

```
angle ← 45.
```

That's why languages such as Pascal and MathCad adopted the symbol combination ":=", as in

```
angle := 45.;
```

to explicitly distinguish assignment from equality.

Why is this distinction important? Well, for one thing, assignment statements must always have a single variable on the left side of the equals sign. Because they both violate this rule, the following legitimate algebraic equations would be invalid as VBA statements:

```
a + b = c
3 = x - y + 99
```

On the other hand, although the following statement is not a proper algebraic equation, it is a perfectly valid assignment statement:

```
x = x + 1
```

After this statement was executed, the memory location for the variable x would have a value that was one higher than its previous value.

Of course, computers also have to process information other than numbers. For example, they must be able to handle names, labels, and identification numbers, which consist of letters, numbers, and symbols. Such *alphanumerical* information is formally referred to as a *string*. In VBA, *string constants* are enclosed in quotes. The variables in which they are stored are called *string variables*. Here's an example of an assignment of a string constant, "Louis Armstrong", to a string variable, n:

```
n = "Louis Armstrong"
```

After this line is executed, a memory location called n will be set up containing the string constant "Louis Armstrong".

1.3 DECISIONS AND LOOPS

To this point, we understand that a program is a *sequence* of unambiguous instructions that the computer implements one after another. In reality, this statement should be amended to read "A program is a sequence of unambiguous instructions that the computer implements one after another, *unless you instruct it to do otherwise.*"

There are two ways in which you can make a program deviate from its sequential mode of operation: decisions and loops. These constructs allow you to vastly increase a program's power to solve numerical problems. In fact, computer scientists have proven that any numerical calculation can be implemented by some combination of sequences, decisions, and loops.

1.3.1   Decisions

As the name implies, a *decision* involves implementing a statement, depending on the outcome of a decision. The *If/Then* statement is the simplest means of implementing decisions in VBA.

Suppose that you want to determine the absolute value of a number. If the number is greater than or equal to zero, you do not have to do anything. However, for a negative number, you would have to make the sign positive. An If/Then statement can be used for this purpose, as in the code

```
If a < 0 Then
    a = -a
End if
```

Because VBA was designed to be easy to understand, the meaning of this If/Then statement is pretty straightforward. In fact, you can read it as if it were an English sentence: "If a is less than zero, then set a equal to its negative." Because of the nature of assignment, this results in the absolute value being generated and stored in the memory location for a.

In addition to generating a single action, a decision can be used to implement one action if a statement is true and another if it is false. Suppose that you want to determine the sign of a number. The following *If/Then/Else* statement can be used for this purpose:

```
If a < 0 Then
    s = -1
Else
    s = 1
End if
```

If a is less than zero, s will be assigned a value of –1, which is mathematically equivalent to a negative sign. If a is not greater than zero (that is it is less than or equal to zero), s will be assigned a value of 1.

1.3.2   Loops

A *loop* repeats a VBA statement (or statements) several times. The *For/Next loop* is the simplest way to do this.

Suppose that you want to calculate the sum of the first n positive whole numbers. A For/Next loop can be used for this purpose:

```
  x = 0
  For i = 1 to n
      x = x + i
  Next i
```

Because VBA is so easy to understand, you should be able to deduce what's going on here. Suppose that n is assigned a value of 5. After x is assigned a value of 0, the actual loop begins with the For statement, wherein the variable i is initially set to 1. The program then moves to the following line, in which x + i is assigned to x. Since i is equal to 1, x would then be equal to 1. At the Next statement, the computer increments i by 1 so that i becomes 2. The computer then transfers control back to the For statement, where VBA determines whether i is greater than n (i.e., 5). If so, VBA exits the loop by transferring to the line immediately following the Next statement. If not, it repeats the body of the loop, so that x becomes 3. The process is repeated until i is greater than n. In our example, x would be equal to 15 and the loop would be terminated.

1.4   A SIMPLE EXAMPLE

Let's tie together the topics of this chapter by writing a simple program to determine either (*a*) the sum of *n* numbers or (*b*) *n!* (that is, *n* factorial), depending on a decision. First, let's figure out how to use a loop to determine a factorial. Recall that

$$n! = 1 \times 2 \times 3 \times ... \times n{-}1 \times n.$$

A *For/Next loop* can be used for this purpose:

```
  x = 1
  For i = 1 to n
    x = x * i
  Next i
```

Notice how this kind of loop differs from the summation loop we described in the last section. Rather than setting the initial value for x to 0, we set it to 1. Otherwise, the loop would always result in x = 0. In addition, the interior of the loop performs multiplication, as is appropriate in computing a factorial.

Along with the summation loop, this loop can be integrated into an If/Then/Else decision:

```
calctype = "summation"
n = 5
If calctype = "summation" Then
  x = 0
  For i = 1 To n
    x = x + i
  Next i
Else
  x = 1
  For i = 1 To n
    x = x * i
  Next i
End If
```

Because we have set `calctype` equal to "summation", the If/Then statement will be true, and the summation loop will be implemented. Therefore, x will be equal to 1 + 2 + 3 + 4 + 5 = 15. Now, suppose that we set `calctype = "factorial"` and n = 4. Then the If/Then statement would be false, and the Else option would be implemented. That is, x would be computed as 1 × 2 × 3 × 4 = 24.

Although this is a pretty simple example, it serves to illustrate how sequences, decisions, and loops can be combined to tell the computer to perform some calculations. If you are new to programming, understanding the material in this chapter is your launching point to understanding how to develop programs of great complexity and value.

KEY TERMS

Alphanumerical	If/Then /Else statement	String
Constant	Loops	String constants
Decision	Program	String variables
For/Next loop	Sequence	Variable
If/Then statement	Statements	

Problems

1. Suppose that we have a cylindrical tank (Figure 1.3) with radius r (m) and height h (m). If the tank is being filled at a flow rate F (m³/min) for a period of time t (min), write a computer program to determine whether it overtops. The program should consist of the following steps:

   - Assign values to the system parameters. In this case, use $r = 5$ m, $h = 10$ m, $F = 15$ m³/min, and $t = 1$ hr.
   - Compute the volume V of the cylinder.
   - Compute the volume V_t of water flowing into the tank over time t.
   - If the tank overflows, compute the volume of water that is lost, and assign it to the variable V_o. Otherwise, set $V_o = 0$.

   Note: x^2 is expressed in VBA as x ^ 2.

2. Set up a simple addition program to do the following:

   - Assign two values to be added to the variables x and y. (Use 532 and 1679.)
   - Assign a value to the variable c_g for a "guess" at the summation. (Use 2133.)
   - Compute the summation and assign the result to the variable c.
   - If the guess is correct, set the variable $g = 1$. Otherwise, set $g = 0$.

3. Write a program to do the following:

   - Assign a value to the variable n. For this case set $n = 7$.
   - Compute the sum of the squares, ss, of the first n positive whole number. After performing the summation, if ss is less than 100, set $ss = 100$.

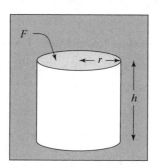

Figure 1.3. A cylindrical tank being filled with a liquid.

2

Overview of VBA for Excel

I'm a firm believer in stepping back and taking in the whole forest before examining individual trees. This is especially important for VBA because of its relationship to the larger world of Microsoft Excel.

Consequently, this chapter is designed to introduce you to how Excel and VBA work in tandem to solve quantitative problems. My main objective is to illustrate how simple it is to design your own interface to implement a rudimentary numerical problem. In addition, I will also introduce some special features of VBA that facilitate obtaining information and displaying results.

Of course, the "devil's in the details" and that's what the rest of the book is for. But for now, let's just enjoy comprehending the big picture and appreciating its value.

OBJECTIVES

After reading this chapter, you should be able to

- Understand the Excel/VBA environment.
- Use Excel as an interface program with VBA.
- Use VBA macros to interface with Excel.
- Understand other VBA statements that obtain and display information.

2.1   THE EXCEL/VBA ENVIRONMENT

Many individuals think that Excel consists exclusively of the worksheets and charts that make up an Excel workbook. As depicted in Figure 2.1, these people are missing half the picture.

An Excel application consists of two separate, but interconnected, environments. One is the familiar workbook environment (Figure 2.1*a*). The other is the *Visual Basic Editor,* or *VBE* (Figure 2.1*b*). The interconnecting arrows show that these two environments work together in an application, and, to do so, they must share and transfer information. To make this all work, then, we have to learn three different disciplines:

1.   Spreadsheet problem-solving

2.   VBA macro programming

3.   Communication between the two environments

You should already have a good grip on the spreadsheet part. We will deal with the last two in this chapter.

2.2   AN EXCEL INTERFACE AND A VBA MACRO PROGRAM

Let's see how VBA and Excel can be used to solve a very simple problem: adding two numbers together and displaying the result. We've chosen such a simple problem to show you how Excel/VBA works without a lot of complicating details. In addition, because active participation is a far better learning approach than passive listening, a hands-on example will be used to instruct you. So before proceeding, turn on your computer and fire up Excel.

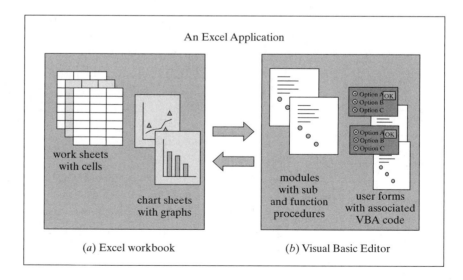

(a) Excel workbook   *(b)* Visual Basic Editor

Figure 2.1.   The two worlds of an Excel application.

2.2.1 Hands-on Exercise: A Simple Addition Program

STEP 1: Start up a new Excel workbook and enter the following information on Sheet1:

Title and authorship information is included at the top of the sheet. Obviously, you should fill in your own information in these cells.

Cells are set up where the user can enter the two numbers to be added (B7 and B8), and the total is displayed (B10). Before proceeding, save the workbook as *SimpleAdder.xls*.

STEP 2: The next step is to write the VBA macro that will get the two values, perform the addition, and output the result. To do this, you have to switch over to the Visual Basic Editor (VBE). There are a couple ways to do this. The easiest is a shortcut key combination, Alt–F11. An alternative is to make the following menu selections: **Tools**, **Macro**, **Visual Basic Editor**.

Either of these approaches should switch you over to the VBE. Once launched, the VBE will be active until it is closed. You can switch back and forth between the two environments with the Alt–F11 combination or with the application tabs at the bottom of the Windows screen. When you save or close the Excel workbook, the VBE will also be saved or closed automatically.

As shown in Figure 2.2, The VBA environment consists of three major areas:

- *The Project Explorer.* This contains the components of your project.

- *The Properties Window.* This contains the properties of the components of your project. We will not make extensive use of the properties window now. However, it is very important when you are working with more advanced features of VBA, such as user forms.

- *The Text Editor.* This is where we will compose our program.

Project Explorer

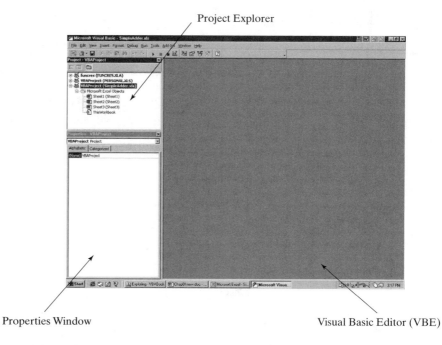

Properties Window   Visual Basic Editor (VBE)

Figure 2.2.   The VBA environment.

Before proceeding, close both the Project Explorer and the Properties windows by clicking on the close buttons on their upper right corners.

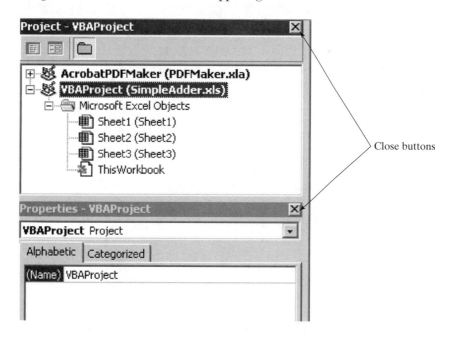

Close buttons

When you do this, the two windows will disappear, and the entire VBE window should be blank. Menu selections can be used to get the windows back. For example, reopen the Project Explorer window, by selecting **View, Project Explorer**. Then reopen the

Properties Window, by selecting **V̲iew, Properties W̲indow**. At this point, you should be back at Figure 2.2.

STEP 3: When you start a new project, the editor will be empty, as shown in Figure 2.2. To actually begin to write a macro, you must first insert a new *module*. In the *Project window*, highlight the project line *VBA Project (SimpleAdder.xls)*.[1] Then make the following menu selections: **I̲nsert, M̲odule**.

A *code* (or *module*) *window* will appear (Figure 2.3). This window is the text editor where you can type your program. If the code window is minimized, you can maximize it to provide "white space" to work in. Also, notice that a new module (*Module1*) is added to your project.

Now, let's write our macro program. Make sure that the cursor is in the code window, and type the following line exactly as shown:

```
sub Adder
```

When you hit enter, the VBE automatically inserts a set of parentheses, skips a space, and adds an End Sub statement

```
Sub Adder()
End Sub
```

This type of macro program is called a *Sub* (short for *sub*routine) *procedure*. The Sub and the End Sub statement are used to establish the beginning and end, respectively, of the procedure. The Sub statement also serves to assign a name to the procedure (in our case, *Adder*). The empty parentheses are referred to as the procedure's *arguments*.

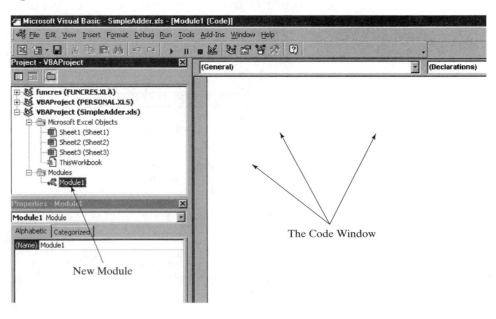

Figure 2.3. A new module along with its corresponding code window.

---

[1] When you have only one workbook open, it's not necessary to highlight the project line before opening a new module. However, it is very important when more than one workbook is open. Thus, highlighting the project line is a good habit to adopt.

Notice that the VBE automatically capitalizes the "s" in Sub and displays both it and the End Sub statement in blue. The editor has a lot of nice features like this to enhance the readability of macros. For example, the following default colors are used:

- *Green* is used for *comments*. These are for labels that start with an apostrophe (for example, `'input data`).
- *Blue* is used for *keywords*. These are words or symbols that are recognized as part of the VBA programming language (for example, Sub and End Sub).
- *Red* is used for statements that contain *syntax errors* (for example, if you erroneously type "Suv" instead of "Sub"). Since the present code has no errors, it contains no red lines. Once you start to write your own programs, you will have many occasions to see this feature.
- *Black* is used for all other text.

STEP 4: Now move the cursor to the line between the Sub Adder() and the End Sub, and type two labels designating your name and today's date:

```
'Ima N. Gineer
'8/05/01
```

It's good programming practice to put such labels throughout your program to document your authorship and to describe what each major segment of code is supposed to do. Notice that VBA automatically makes these labels green so that they stand out.

STEP 5: Next, let's take the first major step in the algorithm: getting the two numbers to be added from the worksheet. To do this, type the following four lines:

```
'input data
Sheets("Sheet1").Select
Range("B7").Select
a = ActiveCell.Value
```

The second line tells VBA that you're interested in doing something on Sheet1, and the third tells it that you are specifically interested in cell B7. The fourth line takes the value in B7 and assigns it to the variable a. At this point, the variable has the value you typed in cell B7. That is, it has a value of 12.

Before proceeding, realize how neat all this is. You now know how to take values that have been entered on a worksheet and bring them into VBA. This means that you've taken the first fundamental step towards learning how to use the worksheet as a user interface for a VBA computational program.

STEP 6: To fetch the second number, we merely mimic what we did for the first number by adding the lines

```
Range("B8").Select
b = ActiveCell.Value
```

Thus, the macro goes to cell B8 and assigns its value (9) to the variable b.

STEP 7: Next, we calculate the summation by simply typing

```
'calculation
c = a + b
```

The sum is assigned to the variable c.

STEP 8: Finally, we perform the last step in the macro algorithm and display the total (c) back on the worksheet. To do this, we type

```
'output results
Range("B10").Select
ActiveCell.Value = c
```

After the comment and the selection of the range, the next line is quite similar to the ones we used to get data from the worksheet into the program. For example, we used the following statement to get the value for the first number:

```
a = ActiveCell.Value
```

We then just reverse the statement to get the total back to the worksheet:

```
ActiveCell.Value = c
```

In other words, we direct Excel to set the value of the selected (i.e., the "active") cell to the result stored in the memory location for c.

At this point, we have a completed program that should look like Figure 2.4. Notice how we have employed blank lines to make the sections of the program easier to discern. This might not be critical for such a simple program, but for larger programs, it makes the code much more readable.

STEP 9: Now that we have set up the macro program, it's time to run it. Using Alt–F11 or clicking the Microsoft Excel tab, go back to Excel. Once you are back in Excel, you have several different ways to run the program. One way is via the menu selections **Tools, Macro, Macros**. This will open a Macro dialogue box, which lists all the macros associated with the current worksheet. At this point, the dialogue box displays the macro you just wrote: Adder. It should be highlighted (if not, select it); then click the Run button, and the macro will execute. If you mistyped something, you will get an error message. Go back to the VBA editor and correct your mistakes until you get the macro to run without errors. Once you do, the worksheet should display the correct result (21) in cell B10.

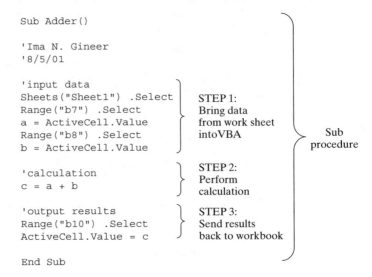

Figure 2.4. Sub procedure to perform simple addition.

STEP 10: A far handier way of running the macro is by creating a button that the user can click. To do that, select **View**, **Toolbars**, **Forms**, and the *forms toolbar* will appear as shown.

Select the redundantly named "button" button ▭, and the pointer will turn into crosshairs. Use these to draw a button by depressing the left mouse button and dragging the crosshairs down and to the right. When you have the right size, release the mouse button. At this point, an *Assign Macro* dialogue box will open:

Select Adder and click OK. Close the Forms toolbar.

To finish off, move the cursor to the interior of the button. The cursor should turn into an editing cursor,[2] which allows you to change the label from Button 1 to something more descriptive, like Run. Change the label, and then click on any work-sheet cell to get out of the Button's edit text mode. At this point, you might also spruce up the work sheet by adding color, shading, etc. If you click on the Run button, the macro will execute, and the worksheet should look something like this:

	A	B	C	D	E
1	**Simple Addition Program**				
2					
3	**Ima N. Gineer**				
4	**Tufts University**				
5	**August 5, 2001**				
6					
7	**First Number**	12		**Run**	
8	**Second Number**	9			
9					
10	**Total**	21			
11					

You have now developed an Excel/VBA interface that will allow you to implement What If? analyses. For example, the user could change the second number to −21 and push the button, and the total would change to −9.

Although Section 2.2.1 is a very simple application, you should recognize that it expresses the fundamental structure of more complicated engineering software. That is, engineers commonly employ algorithms that involve the three-step process of

1. getting data
2. using the data to perform a numerical calculation
3. displaying the results

2.3 OTHER WAYS TO OBTAIN AND DISPLAY INFORMATION

There are two other simple ways to send information between the worksheet and the VBE. The Input Box provides a means of obtaining a single value from the work sheet. Recall that in Section 2.2.1, we obtained the first value to be added with the statements

```
Sheets("Sheet1").Select
Range("B7").Select
a = ActiveCell.Value
```

---

[2] If it doesn't, place the cursor on the button and click the right mouse button. Then select "Edit Text" from the "pull-down menu" that appears.

The *Input Box* can be used for the same purpose:

```
a = InputBox("Please enter the first value to be added")
```

When this statement is executed, the following box will be displayed:

Thus, the user can simply enter the value and click on the OK button in order to assign the value to a.

Note that the input box returns a string constant. Therefore, when entering numerical values, you have to apply the *Val function* to convert the string into a number as in

```
a = Val(InputBox("Please enter the first value to be added"))
```

The *Message Box* provides a handy means of transmitting information back to the user. For example, a simple message can be displayed by

```
MsgBox "This program is designed to add two numbers"
```

Thus, the user can read the message and then click on the OK button to proceed.

In the same fashion, the Message Box can be used to display a numerical result. For example, in Section 2.2.1, we sent the result c back to the worksheet with the code

```
Range("B10").Select
ActiveCell.Value = c
```

The Message Box can be used for the same purpose:

```
Msgbox c
```

When this statement is executed, the following box will be displayed:

Finally, a Message Box can be used to display both a message and a numerical result. For example,

```
MsgBox "The total = " & c
```

will result in the following box being displayed:

The ampersand (&) *concatenates* or "pastes" together the label "The total is" and the value of c to form the complete message.

At this point, you might wonder whether the Message and Input boxes are superior to using worksheet cells. Well, it depends on the problem being solved. For example, if you are inputting only a few values from the sheets, the Input Box might be preferable. But suppose that there are many values to be input. In this case, it would be tedious to make the user enter every single value each time the program was run. In addition, the user might merely want to change one of the input values. In such cases, the worksheet would be the way to go. You will appreciate these trade-offs as you get more experience using VBA.

KEY TERMS

Arguments	Forms toolbar	Range
Alt-F11	Keywords	Sub procedure
Button	Message Box	Syntax errors
Code Window	Module	Text Editor
Comments	Project Explorer	Val function
Concatenates	Project Window	Visual Basic Editor (VBE)
End Sub	Properties Window	

Problems

1. Enhance the simple addition program by having the user enter his or her guess at the correct answer by means of an Input Box. If the guess is correct, have the message box display "Correct result". Otherwise, display the message "Incorrect answer".

2. The volume and the area of the curved surface of a right circular cone (Figure 2.5) can be computed with the following VBA expressions

    ```
    V = 3.141593 * r ^ 2 * h / 3 and A = 3.141593 * r ^ 2 * s
    ```

    where V = volume [m³], r = radius [m], h = height [m], and s = the length [m] of a side of the cone. Design an interface that enters values for r and h on a worksheet. Use a Sub procedure to compute V and A and then display them back on the worksheet. Test the program with $r = 2$ and $h = 4$.

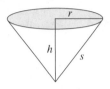

Figure 2.5.

3. The settling velocity of a particle in a liquid can be estimated using *Stokes' law*,

    $$v_s = \alpha \frac{g}{18}\left(\frac{\rho_p - \rho_l}{\mu}\right)d^2,$$

    where v_s = settling velocity [cm s⁻¹], α = a dimensionless form factor reflecting the effect of the particle's shape on the settling velocity (for a sphere, $\alpha = 1.0$), g = the acceleration due to gravity (= 981 cm s⁻²), ρ_p and ρ_l are the densities of the particle and the liquid, respectively [g cm⁻³], μ = dynamic viscosity [g cm⁻¹ s⁻¹], and d = an effective particle diameter [cm]. Design an interface that enters values for α, g, ρ_p, ρ_l, μ, and d in cells on a worksheet. Use a Sub procedure to compute v_s, and display the result with a message box. Test your program for spherical silt particles settling in water: $\rho_p = 2.65$, $\rho_l = 1$, $\mu = 0.014$, and $d = 0.001$ cm. The correct answer is 0.006423 cm/s.

4. If a liquid moves through a pipe at a sufficiently slow velocity, the flow will be smooth, or *laminar*. As the velocity increases, there will come a point at which the flow will become irregular, or *turbulent*. The *Reynolds number* R_e provides a way to determine whether the flow in a pipe is laminar or turbulent. It is calculated as

    $$R_e = \frac{DV}{v},$$

    where D = the pipe's diameter [m], V = the velocity [m s⁻¹], and v = the kinematic viscosity (a measure of the fluid's "thickness") [m²/s]. Note that the velocity can be computed from the flow Q and the pipe's cross-sectional area A_c by $V = Q/A_c$. If R_e is less than 2000, the flow will be laminar. Design an interface that enters values for D, Q, and v. Use a Sub procedure to compute R_e and display it back on the sheet. Use a message box to indicate whether the flow is laminar or turbulent. Test your program for engine oil at 20 °C ($v = 9 \times 10^{-4}$ m²/s) flowing at 0.5 m³/s in a 0.75 m pipe. Use trial-and-error to determine the value of Q that yields $R_e = 2000$.

3

Recording Macros

One way to develop a macro is to write it directly, using VBA. An alternative is to record the macro. When you record a macro, VBA code is automatically generated that corresponds to each step you take as you perform a series of commands in Excel. You can then "play back" the macro to repeat the commands.

The two major purposes for recording macros are as follows:

- **To automate a sequence of Excel commands that you find yourself repeating over and over again.** This was the original reason for recording macros. For example, you may find yourself repeatedly reformatting ranges of cells in a particular way. This is the signal to record a *keystroke macro*. In that way, a series of commands is replaced by a macro that can be invoked with a single key combination.

- **To learn how to write VBA code to control the behavior of a worksheet.** For example, suppose that you want to learn how to write VBA code to reformat a worksheet cell so that it contains boldface type. By recording a macro, VBA code will be generated to accomplish this objective. The code could then be integrated into other programs.

OBJECTIVES

After reading this chapter, you should be able to

- Understand macro recording.
- Understand absolute and relatives references.
- Use macro recording to learn about VBA.
- Understand what keyboard macros can and can't do.

3.1   MACRO RECORDING

In the following exercise, we'll describe how to automate Excel commands and then implement them with a single key combination.

3.1.1   Hands-on Exercise: Macro Recording to Format a Range of Cells

Let's say you wish to create a macro to format a number in a cell so that scientific notation with two digits to the right of the decimal is displayed. We'll use macro recording to do this and then observe the Visual Basic program that is automatically created.

STEP 1: Open a new workbook. Before doing anything else, save it as *SciFormat.xls*. Enter the number 23 in cell B2, and keep that cell selected as the active cell.

STEP 2: Select the menu command **Tools, Macro, Record New Macro**, and a Record Macro dialog box will appear (Figure 3.1). Enter *SciTwoDec* as the macro name. Enter the letter *S* (capital letter) in the shortcut key field, and add a description that will remind you what the macro is supposed to accomplish.

STEP 3: Now select the OK button. Note the Recording flag in the status panel at the lower left of the screen. In addition, somewhere on your screen you should see a small *stop recording button* and a *relative reference button*:[1]

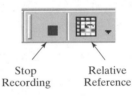

Stop
Recording

Relative
Reference

In this exercise, we'll be using only the *stop recording button*. In the next section, we'll describe the utility of the relative reference button.

Figure 3.1.   The Record Macro dialogue box.

[1] If these do not appear, you can always make them visible with the menu selection **View, Toolbars, Visual Basic**.

STEP 4: Go carefully through the steps required to reformat the number in the cell. An easy way to do this is to right-click on the cell and select *Format Cells*. Then click on the *Number* tab, select *Scientific* from the list on the left, and make certain that 2 is in the Decimal places field. Click OK. Then click the *stop recording button*.

STEP 5: Test whether your macro has been created. Put a number in another cell, and with that cell active (highlighted), press Ctrl–Shift–s. Did the macro work?

Now, let's take a look at the macro that was actually created in Visual Basic. Use the Alt–F11 key combination or the menu selection **Tools, Macro, Visual Basic Editor** to switch over to the Visual Basic Editor. Once you do this, the VBE screen should appear. In the upper left, there should be a *Project—VBA Project window*. This contains the components of your project. There, you should see a Modules entry. Click on the + sign to the left of this entry, and a branch to Module1 should open up. Double-click on the Module1 entry, and a code window should open up on the right containing the SciTwoDec macro:

```
Sub SciTwoDec()
'
' SciTwoDec Macro
' Macro recorded 10/22/2001 by Steve Chapra
' to convert to scientific notation with two decimals
'
' Keyboard Shortcut: Ctrl+Shift+S
'
    Selection.NumberFormat = "0.00E+00"
End Sub
```

The macro recorder has created a VBA Sub procedure called SciTwoDec with no arguments (signified by the empty parentheses).

After a few comments that give the title, date recorded, and shortcut key, the macro program has only one statement (Figure 3.2) that actually does something back on the worksheet. This statement can be broken down as follows:

`Selection`	This pertains to the current cell or cells that are selected.
`NumberFormat`	This is the *property* of the cells that contains the format code as a string constant.
`= "0.00E+00"`	This means that we have an assignment statement wherein the expression on the right of the equals sign—in this case, the string format code `"0.00E+00"`—is assigned to the variable on the left of the equals sign.

So, in one statement, the format of the selected cell(s) is set to scientific notation with two decimal places. That certainly no longer represents literally the sequence of keystrokes that we executed, but it gets the same job done—and more efficiently.

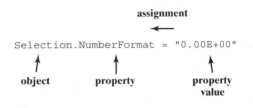

```
                         assignment
                            ←
Selection.NumberFormat = "0.00E+00"
          ↑              ↑          ↑
       object         property   property
                                   value
```

Figure 3.2.   This assignment statement sets the number format of a cell (or cells) to scientific notation with two decimal places.

To test your macro further, go back to the workbook and enter several numbers in cells B4:C6. Then select the block and run your Ctrl–S macro.

There are, of course, many keystroke macros that you might want to create, including, perhaps the following:

- direct text entry   text strings that recur time and time again
- menu commands   common menu command sequences
- editing operations   modifying cell entries and sorting tables
- movement   moving around the work sheet (e.g., to specific locations)
- output   printing out parts of your workbook with specific formatting

You should readily recognize when to create a keystroke macro. Whenever you realize that you are frequently repeating a sequence of keystrokes, you should consider creating a macro. If your macro tends to recur from one workbook to the next, you should store it in your Personal Macro Workbook, which can be selected on the Record New Macro dialog button.

Finally, you should be aware that in standard Excel there are already shortcut keys you can use to perform frequently recurring actions. For example, *Ctrl–s saves* the workbook, and *Ctrl–p* displays the Print dialog box. When you use the same combination of shortcut keys for a recorded macro, the macro will override the default Excel shortcut keys while the workbook that contains the macro is open. Therefore, in selecting your macro shortcut keys, you should avoid frequently used built-in key combinations.

3.2 ABSOLUTE AND RELATIVE REFERENCES

Recall that when we began to record our macro, two buttons appeared:

The one on the right is the *relative reference button*. If you don't click this button before recording, Excel will employ *absolute cell references*. This means that the macro will always record the same action at the same position every time it is executed. Although you often want to do just that, on many other occasions you will want the macro to be implemented relative to the current position of the active cell. The next Hands-on Exercise shows how this is done.

3.2.1 Hands-on Exercise: Absolute versus Relative Recording Mode

You may frequently want to enter your *signature* (i.e., your name, your address, the date, etc., on your spreadsheets. For example, when I develop my programs, I often make the following entries near the top of a new worksheet:

	A	B	C
1			
2			
3	**Steve Chapra**		
4	Civil and Environ. Engrg. Dept.		
5	Tufts University		
6	Medford, MA 02155		
7	10/22/2001 8:05		

STEP 1: Open a new worksheet and save it as *AbsSig.xls*. Before proceeding, get out a piece of paper and write down a similar five-line signature for yourself.

STEP 2: Next, select **Tools, Macro, Record New Macro** from the menu. Enter Absolute as the macro name and the letter *A* (capital letter) in the field after the Ctrl+. Select the OK button.

STEP 3: Implement the following steps (but of course, using your own signature in place of mine):

- Select cell A3 (do this even if it is already selected), and make the following entries

  A3: Steve Chapra
  A4: Civil and Environ. Engrg. Dept.
  A5: Tufts University
  A6: Medford, MA 02155
  A7: =now()

- Select cell A3 and make it boldface
- Click on the *stop recording* button.

STEP 4: Now test whether your macro has been created. Erase the signature, move to cell D10, and press Ctrl–Shift–a. At this point, the macro should write your signature, starting in cell A3. Repeat, but invoke the macro from cell F15. Again, it should begin writing your signature in cell A3.

Press Alt–F11 and examine the macro that was created:

```
Sub Absolute()
'
' Absolute Macro
' Macro recorded 7/24/2000 by Steve Chapra
'
' Keyboard Shortcut: Ctrl+Shift+A
'
    Range("A3").Select
    ActiveCell.FormulaR1C1 = "Steve Chapra"
    Range("A4").Select
    ActiveCell.FormulaR1C1 = "Civil and Environ. Engrg. Dept."
    Range("A5").Select
    ActiveCell.FormulaR1C1 = "Tufts University"
    Range("A6").Select
    ActiveCell.FormulaR1C1 = "Medford, MA 02155"
    Range("A7").Select
    ActiveCell.FormulaR1C1 = "=NOW()"
    Range("A3").Select
    Selection.Font.Bold = True
End Sub
```

Notice how the macro selects each cell explicitly. That is, it starts at cell A3, then selects cell A4, and so on. This is why, regardless of where we had the active cell, the macro always enters the signature in cells A3:A7. As we said previously, this is because we used absolute references.

STEP 5: Suppose, however, that you wanted to add the signature starting somewhere other than in cell A3. For example, you might choose to start it in cell B1. In another application, you might want to start it in cell L3508. This requires that you record the macro in relative mode.

To do this, go back to Excel, save the file, and then close it. Open a new worksheet and save it as *RelSig.xls*. Next, select cell F3. (It doesn't matter which cell you select, as long as you select it prior to starting the macro.) Then start to record a new macro. Enter RelSignature as the macro name, and enter a lowercase *r* in the field after the Ctrl+. Because we might want to invoke this macro in other workbooks, store it in your Personal Macro Workbook, and select the OK button.

STEP 6: Now, before entering the signature, click the *relative reference button* ⊞ to change the recording mode to relative. (When the button is selected, it will appear pressed ⊞ .) Then enter your signature in cells F3:F7, make cell F3 bold, and click the *stop recording* button.

STEP 7: Select cell A3, and press Ctrl–r. At this point, the macro should write your signature starting in cell A3. Now repeat the macro, but invoke it from cell F1. In this case, it will begin writing your signature in cell F1. Thus, the macro is relative.

STEP 8: Press Alt–F11, and now recognize that a new project called Personal.XLS has appeared in the Project—VBA Project Window. This is where your Personal Macro Workbook is stored. Within this project, you should find a Module1, which looks like this:

```
Sub RelSignature()
'
' RelSignature Macro
' Macro recorded 7/24/2000 by Steve Chapra
'
' Keyboard Shortcut: Ctrl+r
'
    ActiveCell.FormulaR1C1 = "Steve Chapra"
    ActiveCell.Offset(1, 0).Range("A1").Select
    ActiveCell.FormulaR1C1 = "Civil and Environ. Engrg. Dept."
    ActiveCell.Offset(1, 0).Range("A1").Select
    ActiveCell.FormulaR1C1 = "Tufts University"
    ActiveCell.Offset(1, 0).Range("A1").Select
    ActiveCell.FormulaR1C1 = "Medford, MA 02155"
    ActiveCell.Offset(1, 0).Range("A1").Select
    ActiveCell.FormulaR1C1 = "=NOW()"
    ActiveCell.Offset(-4, 0).Range("A1").Select
    Selection.Font.Bold = True
End Sub
```

Observe how this version differs from the previous one. For example, rather than first selecting a cell, it merely begins entering the signature starting at ActiveCell. Also, observe the references to cell A1, even though we never went near A1 when we recorded the macro! This is an idiosyncrasy of the recorder, which tends to generate code that is more complicated than is necessary. For example, we can actually remove all the references to A1. The statement

```
ActiveCell.Offset(1, 0).Range("A1").Select
```

could be simplified to

```
ActiveCell.Offset(1, 0).Select
```

and the code will still work properly.

STEP 9: As a final step in this exercise, save and close your workbook and open a new one. Select cell A2 and strike Ctrl–r. Thus, the capability of creating a signature is stored in your Personal Macro Workbook and can be invoked whenever you need it.

The steps in setting up a macro can be summarized as follows:

1. Think about what you want the macro to do.
2. Get things set up properly.
3. Do you want to use relative or absolute modes?
4. Choose **Tools, Macro, Record New Macro**.
5. Enter a name, shortcut key, macro location, and description.
6. Click OK in the Record Macro dialogue box.
7. Select relative or absolute.
8. Perform the actions you want to record, via either pointing (with the mouse) or typing (with the keyboard).
9. After you're finished, click the *stop recording* button on the miniature toolbar.

3.3 USING MACRO RECORDING TO LEARN ABOUT VBA

One of the real advantages of macro recording is that it provides a great vehicle for learning about VBA. For example, in the previous section, we discovered that once we select a cell, its contents can be converted to boldface type by means of the code

```
Selection.Font.Bold = True
```

We can now use this line in another program to make the same conversion. For example, at the beginning of this chapter, we developed the macro SciTwoDec to convert a number in a cell to scientific notation. We can now modify that macro so that it also makes the number boldface. We simply write (we've highlighted the added lines)

```
Sub SciTwoDec()
'
' SciTwoDec Macro
' Macro recorded 7/24/2000 by Steve Chapra
' to convert to scientific notation with two decimals
' and in boldface
'
' Keyboard Shortcut: Ctrl+Shift+S
'
    Selection.NumberFormat = "0.00E+00"
    Selection.Font.Bold = True
End Sub
```

A word of caution regarding macro recording as a learning tool: Oftentimes, the recorder will generate a lot of extraneous code that is not necessary to implement the desired task. Therefore, more often than not, you can develop simpler code to perform the same action. Nevertheless, macro recording provides a powerful means of learning how to do things with VBA.

3.3.1 Hands-on Exercise: Using a Macro Recording to Learn How to Count Data

Let's record a macro to count the number of data in a column of numbers of arbitrary length. That is, the user can put a different number of values in on each run.

STEP 1: Close all applications and then open a new Excel workbook. Save the workbook as *CountMacro.xls*. Enter the following information on Sheet1:

	A	B	C
1			
2			
3			
4	1	36	
5	2	62	
6	3	56	
7	4	43	
8	5	44	
9	6	78	
10	7	40	
11	8	56	
12	9	69	
13	10	62	
14	11	83	
15			

STEP 2: Now, before recording, we have to think about how we might count the numbers in column 2. If we knew the column numbers of the first and last entries we could determine the count of numbers in column 2 by subtracting the former from the latter, as in number of rows = last row – first row + 1. But how *do* we get the column numbers? The value stored in a cell can be accessed by

```
ActiveCell.Value
```

A similar expression that tells you the column of a cell is

```
ActiveCell.Column
```

This approach to getting the attributes or properties of an object (in this case, the column number) is called *object-oriented programming*.

The information thus obtained can be used to count the cells. Before doing so, however, we have to determine how to select the first and the last cells in the column. If, as is often the case, the first value is always in the same location, you could merely use the statement

```
Range("B4").Select
```

The last value is harder, because its location is arbitrary. The easiest way to find it would be to strike the End key followed by the down-arrow key (↓). Let's record a macro to see how VBA does this.

STEP 3: Place the cursor in the cell B4. Start to record a new macro by invoking **Tools, Macro, Record New Macro**. Name the macro "EndDown" and enter a capital letter *E* in the field after the Ctrl+. Click the *relative reference button* to change the recording mode to relative. Now strike the End key followed by the down-arrow key (↓). Click the *stop recording button*. Go to the VBE and view the code that has been created:

```
Sub EndDown()
'
```

```
' EndDown Macro
' Macro recorded 8/13/2001 by Steve Chapra
'
' Keyboard Shortcut: Ctrl+Shift+E
'
    Selection.End(xlDown).Select
End Sub
```

The highlighted line provides the means of going to the last entry in the column.

STEP 4: Open a new module and write the following code:

```
Sub CountCells()
'determine number of data
Range("b4").Select
nr = ActiveCell.Row
Selection.End(xlDown).Select
nr = ActiveCell.Row - nr + 1
Range("b4").Select
'display number of data
MsgBox nr
End Sub
```

As can be seen, the active cell is positioned at the top of the column. Its row number is stored in the variable nr. The next line moves to the last element, where the number of values is calculated and stored in nr. Finally, a *Msgbox statement* provides a simple means of displaying the result. When the program is run, the correct result is displayed.

```
Microsoft Excel   [X]

    11


        OK
```

3.4   WHAT KEYBOARD MACROS CAN'T DO

Although keyboard macros are well worth learning, they are limited. In particular, they cannot do the following:

- Perform repetitive looping
- Perform conditional actions—that is, take different actions, depending on whether something is true or false.
- Assign values to variables
- Specify data types—that is, the type of information stored in a variable. (For example, variables can store integers, decimal numbers, names and labels, etc.)
- Display pop-up messages
- Display custom dialogue boxes

All these limitations can be overcome by writing your own macros in VBA. The remainder of this book will show how that is done.

KEY TERMS

Absolute cell references	Msgbox statement	Relative reference button
Ctrl-p	Object-oriented programming (OOP)	Stop recording button
Ctrl-s	Property	
Keystroke macro	Random Numbers	

Problems

1. Develop a relative macro to turn the fill color of a range of cells red.

2. Record a macro to determine a VBA statement that will count the number of data in a row of numbers of arbitrary length.

3. It is common to use Excel to sort a column of numbers or names. Open a new workbook and type =rand() into cell A1. Then copy the formula to the range from A1:A30. The numbers that appear in these cells are called *random numbers*. They fall between 0 and 1 in a totally random fashion. Hit the recalc key (F9) several times, and see how they automatically change. Such numbers are used in a number of engineering applications, as well as popular applications such as computer games and gambling programs.

   Every time you enter something anywhere on the worksheet, these numbers will change. For the present application, we want to fix their values. So highlight A1:A30 and select **Edit, Copy** and then **Edit, Paste Special,** and then select the radio button for Values and OK. Now hit F9 and notice that nothing happens. Go to cell A1 and notice that the formula =rand() has been transformed to a numeric value.

   Develop a keyboard macro to sort this column in ascending order. After selecting the range of cells, the sort is implemented by making the menu selection **Data, Sort**. A dialogue box will then open that allows you to do a simple "vanilla" sort (one column in ascending order), you should only have to select OK. This will result in the values being sorted.

   Name the macro *Sorter* and assign the shortcut key X (uppercase) to it. Accordingly, it will be invoked by Ctrl–Shift–x. Once you start recording, make certain that you are in relative reference mode before selecting the **Data, Sort** menu selections. Also, design the macro so that the user places the cursor in the top cell so that it sorts an arbitrary number of cells.

   Test your macro by developing another set of random numbers in column C (C1:C25). Make sure to change these random numbers into values prior to applying your keyboard macro to sort them. Finally, type ten first names (for example, your family members and friends) into cells D1:D10 and use your macro to sort these in ascending order.

4

Customized Worksheet Functions

As you know, Excel has many built-in functions. For example, the square root and the arctangent can be evaluated with the SQRT and ATAN functions. Although these provide a wide range of capabilities, there are many engineering-oriented functions that are not available in Excel. Further, there are many instances where you might need to develop your own specially designed functions. The present chapter shows how VBA macros can be used to develop such customized worksheet functions.

Before showing how this is done, I will describe how computer functions are related to mathematical and graphical functions. This is important because of the critical importance of functions in computer programming. Then, I've developed a hands-on exercise to illustrate how a customized function can be implemented to solve a simple engineering problem with Excel/VBA.

OBJECTIVES

After reading this chapter, you should be able to

- Understand the "idea" of a function and how a function is used.
- Recognize and use worksheet function macros.

4.1   THE "IDEA" OF A FUNCTION

There are three related examples of functions: mathematical, graphical, and computer functions. The most familiar is the mathematical function.

Suppose that a parachutist jumps from a stationary platform. Until the rip cord is pulled, the jumper's velocity can be computed with the function

$$v(t) = v_0 e^{-(c_d/m)t} + \frac{gm}{c_d}\left(1 - e^{-(c_d/m)t}\right), \tag{4-1}$$

where $v(t)$ is the downward velocity [m/s], v_0 is the initial downward velocity, t = time [s], g is the gravitational constant [$\cong 9.8$ m/s^2], m is the jumper's mass [kg], and c_d is a proportionality constant called the drag coefficient [kg/s], which parameterizes air resistance.

Now let's talk about the terms in Eq. 4.1. Velocity and time are referred to as the *dependent* and the *independent variable*, respectively. The parenthetical term (t) is appended to v to reinforce this cause–effect relationship. It signifies that v is a function of t; that is, the value of v depends on the value of t. The remaining terms—g, m, c_d, and v_0—are called *parameters*.

If we have values for the parameters (say, $g = 9.8$ m/s^2, $m = 68.1$ kg, $c_d = 12.5$ kg/s, and $v_0 = 0$ m/s), we can plug them into the function to compute the jumper's velocity at a particular time. For example, we might have

$$v(6) = 0e^{-(12.5/68.1)6} + \frac{9.8(68.1)}{12.5}\left(1 - e^{-(12.5/68.1)6}\right) = 35.64 \text{ m/s}.$$

Thus, the function allows us to learn that, after falling for 6 s, the jumper will have a downward velocity of 35.64 m/s. If we desire the jumper's velocity at a different time, we merely plug it into the function and compute a new value of $v(t)$.

Functions can also be displayed graphically. To do this, we merely use the function to generate a table of times and velocities. In the case of Eq. 4.1, we would have the following table:

t, s	v, m/s
0	0.00
2	16.40
4	27.77
6	35.64
8	41.10
10	44.87
12	47.49
∞	53.39

We can then plot the dependent variable as the *ordinate* (y-axis) and the independent variable as the *abscissa* (x-axis) to yield a graphical representation of the function. (See Figure 4.1.)

This graphical representation differs from the equation by providing a global perspective on the functional relationship. Rather than obtaining a velocity for a specific time, it allows us to see all the velocities at a single glance. In this case, we can see that the model makes sense. As we would expect, the parachutist accelerates because the downward velocity is initially small and, therefore, air resistance is minimal. However, as

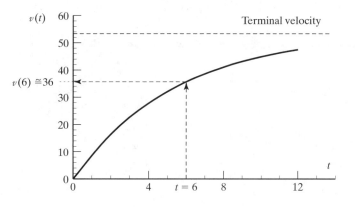

Figure 4.1.   The velocity of a falling parachutist as a function of time.

the velocity increases, the parachutist's acceleration decreases. After a sufficiently long time, a constant velocity is approached. This terminal velocity occurs because the downward force of gravity is in balance with the upward force of air resistance.

Of course, graphs can be used to make a single prediction, as depicted in the figure for the case of $t = 6$. But obviously, the result is known to less precision than could be obtained with a mathematical function evaluated with the use of a calculator or computer.

The bottom line is that both the mathematical and graphical functions provide the same benefit. That is, we can send both functions information ($t = 6$), and they return a single result ($v \cong 36$ m/s).

This is precisely the role of computer functions. The simplest examples are the built-in Excel functions like SQRT, ABS, SIN, etc. If we want to evaluate $\sqrt{9}$, we merely go to a cell and type in

=SQRT(9)

When we hit enter, the result, 3, appears in the cell. So just like the mathematical and graphical functions, we pass some information (9) to the function through its argument, and the function sends us back a result (3).

4.2   WORKSHEET FUNCTION MACROS

Although the built-in Excel functions provide great capabilities, they are sometimes not adequate for certain engineering problems. In such cases, *worksheet function macros* provide a means of creating your own custom-designed functions. In the next Hands-on session, we'll show you how to build and implement such a macro.

4.2.1   Hands-on Exercise: A Simple Worksheet Function Macro

It is a simple matter to evaluate Eq. 4.1 with Excel. However, suppose that at some arbitrary time into the jump, the parachutist pulls the rip cord. At that point, the drag coefficient would increase, due to the additional air resistance of the open chute. Let's explore how this feature can be added to the falling parachutist model by means of a worksheet function macro.

STEP 1: Open a new Excel work sheet and enter the following information:

	A	B	C
1	Parachutist Problem		
2	Ima N. Gineer		
3	Tufts University		
4	August 14, 2001		
5			
6	g	9.8	m/s2
7	m	68.1	kg
8	cd	12.5	kg/s
9	v0	0	m/s
10	tc	6	s
11	cdp	62.5	kg/s
12			
13	t, s	v (no chute)	v (chute)
14	0		
15	2		
16	4		
17	6		
18	8		
19	10		
20	12		

Notice how we have set up cells to hold the parameter values. In addition, we have added two new parameters: tc = the time at which the rip cord is pulled, and cdp = the drag coefficient after the parachute is deployed. Before proceeding, save the file as *parachutist.xls*.

STEP 2: We can make our subsequent work easier by naming the cells holding the parameters. To do so, select cells A6:B11. (The easiest way to do this is by selecting cell A6, holding down the left mouse button, and dragging the cursor down to B11). Next, make the menu selections **Insert, Name, Create, Left column, OK.**

To verify that this has worked properly, select cell B6 and check that the label "g" appears in the name box (located on the upper left side of the sheet just below the menu bars).

STEP 3: Move to cell B14, and enter the equation for the free-falling parachutist as

```
=v0*EXP(-cd/m*A14)+g*m/cd*(1-EXP(-cd/m*A14))
```

When this formula is entered, the value 0 should appear in cell B14. Then copy the formula down the range B15:B20. Cell B20 should have a value of 47.49. Add an *xy*-plot of *v* (no chute) versus *t*, s. The spreadsheet should look like this:

	A	B	C	D	E	F	G	H
1	Parachutist Problem							
2	Ima N. Gineer							
3	Tufts University							
4	August 14, 2001							
5								
6	g	9.8	m/s2					
7	m	68.1	kg					
8	cd	12.5	kg/s					
9	v0	0	m/s					
10	tc	6	s					
11	cdp	62.5	kg/s					
12								
13	t, s	v (no chute)	v (chute)					
14	0	0.00						
15	2	16.40						
16	4	27.77						
17	6	35.64						
18	8	41.10						
19	10	44.87						
20	12	47.49						

All that we have done so far here is typical of the standard use of Excel. For example, at this point you could change parameter values and see how the analytical solution changes.

STEP 4: We will now illustrate how Visual BASIC macros can be used to extend the standard Excel capabilities. To create a user-defined function, switch over to the Visual Basic Editor with the Alt–F11 key combination. In the *Project—VBA Project window*, highlight the project line *VBA Project (parachutist.xls)*. Insert a module, and type in the following Visual BASIC function:

```
Function Vel(t, g, m, cd, v0, tc, cdp)
'Function to compute velocity of falling parachutist
'before and after pulling the rip cord
't = time, s
'g = gravitational constant, m/s2
'm = mass, kg
'cd = drag coefficient, kg/s
'v0 = initial velocity, m/s
'tc = time when rip cord pulled, s
'cdp = drag coefficient after rip cord pulled, kg/s
If t < tc Then
   'compute velocity for free fall
   Vel = v0 * Exp(-cd / m * t) _
                  + g * m / cd * (1 - Exp(-cd / m * t))
Else
   'compute velocity when parachute is first deployed
   v0p = v0 * Exp(-cd / m * tc) _
                  + g * m / cd * (1 - Exp(-cd / m * tc))
   'compute velocity after parachute is deployed
   Vel = v0p * Exp(-cdp / m * (t - tc)) _
                  + g * m / cdp * (1 - Exp(-cdp / m * (t - tc)))
End If
End Function
```

We have added some new features to this code. First, because the equations are getting a bit long, we have written them on two lines. To do this, we place a space and an underscore in the position at which we want to break the line.

Second, notice that we have included a decision here by using an If/Then/Else construct. Because VBA is such an easy-to-understand language, the construct can be read like a sentence:

If the time is prior to the time when the cord is pulled, *Then*

Compute the fall velocity at time t, using Eq. 4.1 with v0 and cd

Else (i.e., the rip cord has been pulled and the chute deployed)

Compute the initial velocity at the instant the cord is pulled (v0p)

Compute the velocity at times thereafter, using Eq. 4.1 with v0p and cdp

End If

The indentation merely makes the logic of the construct easier to discern.

Finally, notice that the answer is assigned to the name of the function (Vel). This is VBA's way of passing the results back to Excel.

STEP 5: To implement the function, return to the spreadsheet (Press Alt–F11) and enter the following formula into cell C14:

```
=Vel(A14,g,m,cd,v0,tc,cdp)
```

The result 0 will appear in cell C14. When you enter the function into the spreadsheet cell, the argument list (the values in parentheses) is used to pass the parameters into the VBA function Vel. In VBA, the calculations are performed, and the result is then passed back and displayed in the cell. Note that the order of the values in parentheses should be the same as that in the function statement in VBA.

STEP 6: Now copy this formula to the remainder of the cells (C15:C20). Finally, make a plot of the two sets of velocities. The result should look like this:

	A	B	C	D	E	F	G	H
1	Parachutist Problem							
2	Ima N. Gineer							
3	Tufts University							
4	August 14, 2001							
5								
6	g	9.8	m/s2					
7	m	68.1	kg					
8	cd	12.5	kg/s					
9	v0	0	m/s					
10	tc	6	s					
11	cdp	62.5	kg/s					
12								
13	t, s	v (no chute)	v (chute)					
14	0	0.00	0.00					
15	2	16.40	16.40					
16	4	27.77	27.77					
17	6	35.64	35.64					
18	8	41.10	14.66					
19	10	44.87	11.31					
20	12	47.49	10.78					

Notice how the velocity for the "no chute" case continues to increase to a high level (the gray line). In contrast, once the chute opens, the parachutist rapidly decelerates to a terminal velocity of about 10 m/s.

You should appreciate what has happened here. When you enter the function into the spreadsheet cell, the parameters are passed into the Visual BASIC program, where the calculation is performed and the result is then passed back and displayed in the cell. Thus, just like the built-in functions (such as Sin and Sqrt), the customized function Vel is sent information and returns a single result.

KEY TERMS			
Abscissa	End Function	Parameters
Arctangent	Function	Radians
Degrees	Independent Variable	
Dependent Variable	Ordinate	

Problems

1. Develop a macro along the lines of Section 4.2.1, but add a second macro function to compute the number of G's the jumper is being subjected to. A useful quantity because it can be correlated with injuries due to jumping, the number of G's is equal to the acceleration divided by the gravitational constant. Enter this function into column D, and add that column to the plot. Note that the acceleration is merely equal to the balance of downward and upward forces on the parachutist. Therefore, before the rip cord was pulled, the G's would be calculated as

$$G = \frac{g - (c_d / m)v}{g} \qquad (4\text{-}2)$$

2. Set up the following worksheet to solve for the velocity of the falling parachutist (assuming that the initial vertical velocity is zero):

	A	B	C
1	Falling Parachutist Velocity		
2	Ima Student		
3			
4	mass	68.1	kg
5	drag	12.5	kg/s
6	gravity	9.8	m/s2
7	time	10	s
8			
9	velocity		m/s

    (*a*) Write a VBA function named VelCalc that computes the jumper's velocity and passes the value back to the worksheet. (**Note: do not name the cells.**)

    (*b*) What formula would be entered into cell B9 in order to compute the velocity by means of the function procedure?

3. Like most software products, Excel uses **radians** to evaluate its trigonometric functions. However, many individuals are more comfortable using **degrees**. The two measures are related by the fact that 180° are equivalent to π radians. If you wanted to use degrees for an application, you could always imbed the conversion into the argument. For example, you could evaluate the sine of 30 degrees by entering

```
=SIN(30*PI()/180)
```

and the result, 0.5, would appear.[1] But suppose that you wanted to make such evaluations repeatedly and didn't want to bother to include the conversion on every implementation. Develop a macro function called SIND that provides a way to do this.

Note that although you might have memorized the value of π to seven or more significant figures, there is a neat trick to get VBA (or any computer language) to determine it for you. Recall that the tangent of the angle $\pi/4$ (that is, 45°) is 1. Therefore, the arctangent of 1 is equal to $\pi/4$. Consequently, the computer can determine π for you as 4 times the arctangent of 1. In VBA, this can be written as

```
pi = 4 * Atn(1)
```

4.   Develop a VBA function to take the square root of the sum of the squares of two numbers.

5.   Set up the following worksheet:

	A	B	C	D
1	Parachutist Problem			
2				
3	Ima Student			
4	Tufts University			
5	Medford, MA 02155			
6				
7	Parameter	Symbol	Value	Units
8	Mass	m	200	kg
9	Drag coefficient	cd	12.7	kg/s
10	Acceleration of gravity	g	9.8	m/s2
11	Time rip cord pulled	t	10	s
12	Injury velocity	vcrit	65	m/s
13				
14	Velocity	v		m/s

Assign the symbol names to the cells between the arrows

Notice that we have included an injury velocity (vcrit) that corresponds to the velocity at which injuries tend to occur when the rip cord is pulled. Create a macro function called **_Velocity_** to do the following:

- Compute the parachutist's velocity as a function of time, mass, drag, and gravity.

- If the velocity is greater than or equal to the critical velocity, display a message box alerting you that injuries could occur. Here's the code to do this:

```
If Velocity > vcrit Then
   Msg = "Injury Velocity Exceeded"
   Style = vbOKOnly + vbCritical
   Title = "Alert!"
   MsgBox Msg, Style, Title
End If
```

- Enter the function into cell C14. Test the program by trying a mass that should be safe (50 kg). Then try a value that should cause injury (200 kg).

---

[1] The value of π itself can be invoked through a built-in Excel function, PI().

5

Modular Programming

Imagine how difficult it would be to study a textbook that had no chapters, sections, or paragraphs. Breaking complicated tasks or subjects into more manageable parts is one way to make them easier to handle. In the same spirit, computer programs can be divided into small procedures. A *procedure* is a named sequence of statements that are executed as a unit to perform a given task. This approach is called *modular programming*.

The most important attribute of modules is that they be as independent and self-contained as possible. In addition, they are typically designed to perform a specific, well-defined function. As such, they are usually highly focused and short (generally no more than 50 to 100 instructions in length).

Two types of procedure are commonly employed: *Sub* (short for *Subroutine*) *procedures* and *Function procedures*. The former usually returns several results, whereas the latter returns a single result. In VBA, a *calling*, or *main*, Sub procedure invokes the other procedures as they are needed. Thus, the main Sub procedure orchestrates each of the parts in a logical fashion.

OBJECTIVES

After reading this chapter, you should be able to

- Write a procedure with the Visual Basic Editor.
- Run a main Sub procedure with a button.
- Invoke a Sub procedure with a Call statement.
- Invoke a Function procedure with its name.
- Understand the difference between Sub and Function procedures.
- Understand how procedure arguments work.
- Pass variables to procedures by value and by reference.
- Understand how Static variables relate to local variables in procedures.

Modular programming has a number of advantages. The use of small, self-contained units makes the underlying programming logic easier for the developer to construct and the user to understand. Development is facilitated because each procedure can be perfected in isolation. In fact, for large projects, different programmers can work on individual parts. In the same spirit, you can maintain your own library of useful procedures for later use in other programs. Modular programming also increases the ease with which a program can be debugged and, tested because errors can be more easily isolated. Finally, program maintenance and modification are facilitated, primarily because new procedures can be developed to perform additional tasks and then be easily incorporated into the already coherent and organized scheme.

5.1 SUB PROCEDURES

A simplified representation of the syntax for Sub procedures is[1]

```
Sub name ([arglist])
[statements]
[Exit Sub]
[statements]
End Sub
```

where *name* is the name you give to the Sub, *arglist* represents the argument list that is passed to the Sub procedure when it is called (multiple variables are separated by commas), *statements* are any group of statements to be executed within the Sub procedure, and `Exit Sub` is a statement that provides an immediate exit from the procedure prior to its completion. A more compete description of this and other syntax descriptions can be found in the VBA Help facility. For example, if you highlight Sub and press the F1 key, a detailed description, including syntax, exceptions, and examples, will appearon your monitor.

The Sub procedure is invoked by a *Call statement*, which has the syntax

```
Call name([arglist])
```

The Call statement transfers control to the Sub procedure. After the Sub is executed, control returns to the line following the Call statement.

Here's a simple example that uses a Sub to add two numbers:

```
Sub SimpleAddition()
'assign values
a = 15
b = 28
'compute the sum                    The "main" Sub
Call Add(a, b, c)
'display the results
MsgBox c
End Sub

Sub Add(a, b, c)
c = a + b
End Sub
```

---

[1] In these syntax descriptions, we use the same conventions as those you'll find in the VBA help facility. The code written by the programmer is written in italics, and all optional statements are enclosed in brackets. You can obtain a more complete description of the Sub procedure with VBA help.

After assigning values to a and b in the main Sub, the Call transfers control down to `Sub Add`. Here, the addition is performed, the result is assigned to c, and control is transferred back to the main Sub, where a MsgBox is used to display the result. Thus, `Add` is sent information through its argument list (a and b), does a specific job (performs the addition), and then returns the results to the main Sub through its argument list (c). Now let's examine a more interesting example.

5.1.1   Hands-on Exercise: The Kick Calculator

Let's see how a VBA Sub procedure can be used to solve a typical problem from an introductory physics course involving projectile motion. If a projectile is launched at a given velocity v_i and angle θ_i (see Figure 5.1), the initial horizontal (v_{x0}) and vertical (v_{y0}) components of velocity can be computed as

$$v_{x0} = v_i \cos(\theta_i) \tag{5-1}$$

and

$$v_{y0} = v_i \sin(\theta_i). \tag{5-2}$$

If the range is defined as the time required to return to $y = 0$, the travel time and range can be respectively computed as

$$t_r = \frac{2v_{y0}}{g} \tag{5-3}$$

and

$$x_r = v_{x0}t_r. \tag{5-4}$$

Calculations like these are typically used in disciplines such as aerospace engineering. However, they also apply to other areas—one example being sports science, in which the researches may study the effectiveness of kickers in football,[2] soccer, or rugby.

For instance, in American football, the "punter" would be interested in evaluating both the range and the travel time (formally called the "hang time") of his kicks. The range is important because long kicks push the opposing punt returner farther back into his own territory. The long hang time is important because it allows the coverage team time to get downfield and attempt to tackle the returner before he advances.

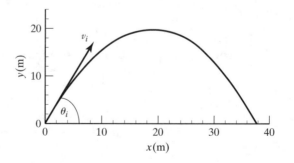

Figure 5.1.   The trajectory of a projectile, showing the initial velocity and angle.

[2] Most of the world uses the term "football" to refer to what we in the U.S. call soccer.

Interestingly, there is a trade-off between these two objectives. If the punter sacrifices hang time for distance, the coverage team might not have sufficient time to get downfield and contain and tackle the returner. (This is called "outkicking your coverage.") Conversely, you can always optimize the hang time by sacrificing distance and kicking the ball straight up into the air!

STEP 1: Start Excel and enter the following information into Sheet1:

	A	B	C
1	Kick Calculator		
2			
3	Ima N. Gineer		
4	Tufts University		
5	August 15, 2001		
6			
7	Parameter	Value	Units
8	Initial speed	23	m/s
9	Initial angle	35	degrees
10			
11	Results:		
12	Hang time		s
13	Range		m

After entering the information, change the name of the worksheet to "Interface" and save the workbook as kicker.xls.

STEP 2: The next step is to create a Sub procedure to compute the hang time and range. Switch over to the Visual Basic Editor (VBE) with the Alt–F11 key combination. Once you are in VBE, insert a module using the menu commands **Insert, Module**.

STEP 3: Now we're going to type in a program a few lines at a time, explaining important points as we proceed. First, type the next line,

```
Sub KickCalc
```

When you hit enter, VBA automatically inserts a set of parentheses, skips a space, and adds an End Sub statement to give

```
Sub KickCalc()
End Sub
```

STEP 4: Now move the cursor to the line between Sub ·KickCalc() and End Sub, and add two comments designating your name and today's date:

```
'Ima N. Gineer
'August 15, 2001
```

It's good programming practice to put comments throughout your program in order to document your authorship and to describe what each major piece of code is supposed to do.

STEP 5: Next, let's take the first real step in the algorithm: getting the initial speed and angle from the worksheet. To do this, type the following four lines:

```
'input data
Sheets("Interface").Select
```

```
Range("b8").Select
vi = ActiveCell.Value
```

The second line tells VBA that you're interested in doing something on the sheet named Interface, and the third tells it that you are specifically interested in cell b8. The fourth line takes the value in b8 and assigns it to the variable vi. At this point, vi has the value you typed in cell b8 (i.e., it has the value 23).

Next, we obviously want to fetch the initial angle. I'm going to show you two ways to do this (I prefer the latter because it's more flexible, so that's the one we'll use here). First, you can mimic what we did for vi by adding the following lines to your program (don't actually type them):

```
Range("b9").Select
ai = ActiveCell.Value
```

Thus, the macro goes to cell b9 and assigns its value (35) to the variable ai.

However, rather than "wiring" in values for b8, b9, etc., an alternative is to tell the computer to merely shift down one cell using the Offset property as in

```
ActiveCell.Offset(1, 0).Select
ai = ActiveCell.Value
```

This is the version you should type into your program

The *Offset property* works on the principle of shifting down a number of rows and to the right a number of columns as expressed by its generic representation,[3]

```
Offset(RowOffset, ColumnOffset)
```

Thus, Offset(1, 0) will shift down one row while staying in the same column (which is precisely what we want to do for the present case). What would Offset(2, -3) do?

Why might the Offset statement be preferred? Suppose that you were entering a large number of parameters and you used specific range selections to input them into VBA. At a later time you might want to insert a new parameter near the top of the list. This would necessitate renumbering all the range selections below the insertion point. On the other hand, because the Offset property is relative to the current selection, you would only have to change the first range selection.

STEP 6: We will now calculate the hang time and the distance. To do this, simply type Eqs. 5.1 through 5.4:

```
'calculation
vx0 = vi * Cos(ai * 3.14159 / 180)
vy0 = vi * Sin(ai * 3.14159 / 180)
tr = 2 * vy0 / 9.81
xr = tr * vx0
```

Hence, the hang time and distance are assigned to the variables tr and xr, respectively. Note that, because all trigonometric functions employ radians, we use the conversion $180°/\pi$ radians in the first two equations.

---

[3] Rows are horizontal and columns are vertical as expressed by the memory aid: "The rows of a church and the columns of a temple."

STEP 7: Finally, we can display the results (`tr` and `xr`) back on the worksheet. To do this, type

```
'output results
Range("b12").Select
ActiveCell.Value = tr
ActiveCell.Offset(1,0).Select
ActiveCell.Value = xr
```

After the comment, the next two lines are quite similar to the ones we used to get data from the worksheet into the program. In other words, we direct Excel to select cells (in this case, `"b12"` and `"b13"`) and then set them to the values of `tr` and `xr`.

At this point, the completed program looks like this:

```
Sub KickCalc()
'Ima N. Gineer
'August 15, 2001
'input data
Sheets("Interface").Select
Range("b8").Select
vi = ActiveCell.Value
ActiveCell.Offset(1,0).Select
ai = ActiveCell.Value
'calculation
vx0 = vi * Cos(ai * 3.14159 / 180)
vy0 = vi * Sin(ai * 3.14159 / 180)
tr = 2 * vy0 / 9.8
xr = tr * vx0
'output results
Range("b12").Select
ActiveCell.Value = tr
ActiveCell.Offset(1,0).Select
ActiveCell.Value = xr
End Sub
```

STEP 8: Now that we have set up the macro program, it's time to run it. Go back to Excel by using Alt–F11. Once back in Excel, you have several different ways to run the program. One way is via the menu selections **Tools, Macro, Macros**. These will open a Macro dialogue box, which lists all the macros associated with the current worksheet. At this point, it displays the one you just wrote: `KickCalc`, which should be highlighted; if it isn't, select it. Then hit the Run button, and the macro will execute. If you mistyped something, you will get an error message. In that case, go back to the VBA editor and correct your mistakes until you get the macro to run without errors. Once you get it to run correctly, the worksheet should display the correct results (`tr = 2.69 s` and `xr = 50.72 m`) in cells `b12` and `b13`.

STEP 9: Although we can certainly run the macro in the manner just described, a far handier way is by creating a button that the user can merely click to run the macro. To do that, select **View, Toolbars, Forms** from the menu bar, and the forms toolbar will appear:

Select the redundantly named "button" button , and the pointer will turn into crosshairs. Draw a button by depressing the left mouse button and dragging the cursor down and to the right. Release the mouse button to complete the process. At this point, an *Assign Macro dialogue box* will open:

Select KickCalc and click OK. Close the forms toolbar. To finish off, move the cursor to the interior of the button. The cursor should turn into an editing pointer,[4] which allows you to change the label from Button 1 to something more descriptive, like Run. Do this, and then click on any worksheet cell to get out of the Button's edit text mode. At this point, you might also spruce up the worksheet by adding color, shading, etc.

---

[4] If it doesn't, place the cursor on the button and click the right mouse button. Then select "Edit Text" from the pull-down menu that appears.

You have now developed an Excel–VBA interface that will permit you to implement "What If...?" analyses. In particular, this interface will allow you to determine the impact of the initial velocity and angle on the hang time and range of a football. To illustrate, change the initial angle to 65° and click on the Run button. The macro should execute and the worksheet should look something like the following:

	A	B	C	D	E	F
1	Kick Calculator					
2						
3	Ima N. Gineer				Run	
4	Tufts University					
5	August 15, 2001					
6						
7	Parameter	Value	Units			
8	Initial speed	23	m/s			
9	Initial angle	65	degrees			
10						
11	Results:					
12	Hang time	4.25	s			
13	Range	41.35	m			
14						

We can see that by increasing the angle, the hang time increases, but the distance decreases.

You can then use the software to examine other cases. For example, you could use it to determine the initial angle that produces the maximum range. Then you could determine whether that optimal angle is independent of the initial velocity.

5.2 FUNCTION PROCEDURES

Like a Sub procedure, a *Function procedure* is a separate procedure that can take arguments and perform a series of statements. However, it differs from a Sub in that (*a*) it is invoked through its name and (*b*) it returns a single value. A simplified representation of the syntax of a Function procedure is

```
Function name ([arglist])
[statements]
[name = expression]
[Exit Function]
[statements]
[name = expression]
End Function
```

where *name* is the name you give to the function, `arglist` represents the argument list that is passed to the function when it is invoked, `statements` are any group of statements to be executed within the function, and `Exit Function` is a statement that provides an immediate exit from the procedure prior to its completion. Notice that a value is returned from a function by assigning the value to the function name. Any number of such assignments can appear anywhere within the function.

You invoke a Function procedure by using the function's name, followed by the argument list in parentheses. Here's a simple example that uses a Function to add two numbers:

```
Sub SimpleAddition()
'assign values
a = 15
b = 28
'compute the sum
c = Add(a, b)
'display the results
MsgBox c
End Sub
Function Add(a, b)
Add = a + b
End Function
```

The "main" Sub

After assigning values to a and b, the function name (Add) causes control to be transferred down to the function. After the addition is performed and the result assigned to the function name, control is transferred back to the main Sub, where the result is assigned to c. A MsgBox is then used to display the result. Thus, the function is sent information via its argument list (a and b), does a specific job (performs the addition), and then returns the results via its name (Add). Consequently, you can use a Function procedure on the right side of an expression in the same way you use any intrinsic function, such as Sqr, Cos, or Abs, when you want to use the value returned by the function.

Because it returns a single value, a Function procedure can also be invoked outside of expressions. For example, the preceding addition example can be simplified as follows:

```
Sub SimpleAddition()
'assign values
a = 15
b = 28
'compute and display the results
MsgBox Add(a, b)
End Sub
Function Add(a, b)
Add = a + b
End Function
```

In this case, Add is invoked as part of the message box.

5.3 MORE ABOUT PROCEDURE ARGUMENTS

The argument list provides a means to control the flow of information between the calling program and the procedure. The procedure's *arguments* are collectively referred to as its *parameter list*, and each argument is called a *parameter*.

The two-way communication between the procedure and the main program is illustrated in Figure 5.2. The subroutine needs data to act on and must return its results, to be utilized in the main program. The data and results are said to be "passed" between the procedures.

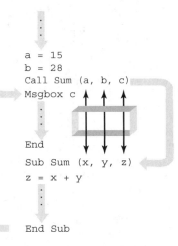

```
a = 15
b = 28
Call Sum (a, b, c)
Msgbox c
     .
     .
     .
End
Sub Sum (x, y, z)
z = x + y
     .
     .
     .
End Sub
```

Figure 5.2. Typical sequence of a SUB procedure call and return. The SUB procedure determines values from the calling program via its parameter list. After execution of the procedure, the value of the sum will be contained in the variable c in the calling program. The parameter list is like a window through which information is selectively passed between the calling program and the procedure.

Notice that the arguments in the calling program may have variable names different from those in the procedure. Although the same names could have been used, different names are employed to highlight the modular nature of a procedure and to reinforce the fact that the two sets of variables can be given different names. This property is illustrated in the next exercise.

5.3.1   Hands-on Exercise: The Behavior of the Parameter List

STEP 1: In this exercise, we investigate how the parameter list controls the flow of information between procedures. Fire up Excel, and open a new workbook called ParamList.xls. Go to the VBE and insert the following module:

```
Sub Test()
a = 1
b = 2
c = 3
MsgBox a & "   " & b & "   " & c & "   " & d
Call Arg(a, b, c)
MsgBox a & "   " & b & "   " & c & "   " & d
End Sub
Sub Arg(b, a, d)
MsgBox a & "   " & b & "   " & c & "   " & d
d = 4
c = b
MsgBox a & "   " & b & "   " & c & "   " & d
End Sub
```

STEP 2: When you run Sub Test, the first Msgbox yields

```
┌─────────────────────────────┐
│ Microsoft Excel        ☒    │
├─────────────────────────────┤
│   1  2  3                   │
│        ┌──────────┐         │
│        │    OK    │         │
│        └──────────┘         │
└─────────────────────────────┘
```

Thus, a, b and c have their original assigned values of 1, 2, and 3, respectively. The variable d is displayed as a blank because it has not been assigned a value.

After the OK button is clicked, the Sub procedure Arg is called. The values of a, b and c are passed to Arg, where they are temporarily associated with the variable names b, a, and d, respectively. Consequently, when the second Msgbox statement is implemented, the result is

```
┌─────────────────────────────┐
│ Microsoft Excel        ☒    │
├─────────────────────────────┤
│   2  1   3                  │
│        ┌──────────┐         │
│        │    OK    │         │
│        └──────────┘         │
└─────────────────────────────┘
```

Therefore, the values that are passed as parameters b, a, and d initially have values related to the variables a, b, and c in the main program. Hence, a = 2, b = 1, and d = 3. Because c does not appear in the parameter list, it has no value within Arg.

After OK is clicked, d is assigned a value of 4 and c is assigned a value of 1 by the statement c = b. The resulting MsgBox is

```
┌─────────────────────────────┐
│ Microsoft Excel        ☒    │
├─────────────────────────────┤
│   2  1  1  4                │
│        ┌──────────┐         │
│        │    OK    │         │
│        └──────────┘         │
└─────────────────────────────┘
```

After OK is clicked now, the results for b, a, and d are passed back to the calling Sub, where they are assigned to a, b and c, respectively. Hence, the final MsgBox is

```
┌─────────────────────────────┐
│ Microsoft Excel        ☒    │
├─────────────────────────────┤
│   1  2  4                   │
│        ┌──────────┐         │
│        │    OK    │         │
│        └──────────┘         │
└─────────────────────────────┘
```

Observe how the value of 4 is assigned to the variable c because of its position in the parameter list. On the other hand, the assignment statement in Arg, d = 4, has no effect on the variable d in the main program. This is because d is not included in the Call parameter list. Therefore, the two d's are distinct.

The foregoing exercise serves to illustrate how the parameter list operates. In particular, it demonstrates how actions and variables in a Sub procedure can be either isolated from or connected to other parts of a program. This property is essential to the implementation of modular programming.

Variables that are used exclusively within a procedure are referred to as *local variables*. In the previous hands-on exercise, the variable c in the Sub Arg was local. Because c is not "passed" back to the main program, the value of c = 1 holds only in Arg and has no effect on the value of c in the main program.

The ability to have local variables in a procedure is a great asset. In essence, they serve to make each subroutine a truly autonomous entity. For example, changing a local variable will have no effect on variables outside the subroutine. As we have seen, local variables can even have the same name as variables in other parts of the program, yet still be distinct entities. One advantage of this feature is that it decreases the likelihood of "side effects" that occur when the value of a global variable is changed inadvertently in a subprogram.

For example, you might use the variable t to represent time in the main Sub. In the called Sub, you might use the same variable name for temperature. If the latter sub represents t as a local variable, you can vary temperature values without worrying whether you have changed the value of time in the main Sub.

Finally, the existence of local variables also facilitates the debugging of a program. Subprograms can be debugged individually without fear that a working subroutine will cease functioning because of an error in another subroutine.

5.4   PASSING BY VALUE OR BY REFERENCE

There will be occasions upon which you may want to perform operations on a variable in a procedure that change the value of the variable. At the same time, you may want to retain the original value for some other purpose. On such occasions, *passing by value* provides a handy means of performing the desired operation while maintaining the integrity of the original variable. To understand how this works, it is useful to examine how memory locations are allocated when a procedure is called.

When a variable appears in a program, a location is defined in the computer's memory. When an action is taken to assign a value to the variable, the value resides at the said location. Now, when a variable name is passed to a procedure via a *Parameter-List*, a new memory location is not created. Rather, the computer goes back to the original memory location designated in the main program in order to obtain the value of the variable. The computer does this because of the presence of the variable in the parameter list. This approach is referred to as passing the parameter *by reference*. In such cases, changing the value of the parameter in the Sub will result in its value being changed in the memory location specified in the main program.

In contrast, suppose that the argument in the parameter list is a constant. For example, if you wanted to pass a value of 2 as the first argument in the Add procedure described earlier, you could merely include the statement

```
Call Add(2, b, c)
```

Because it is a constant, the 2 is copied to a temporary memory location, and the address of that location is passed to the procedure. This approach is referred to as passing the parameter *by value*, and it has special significance because variables can also be passed by value. To do so, we enclose the variable in parentheses. For example, suppose that we wanted to pass the variable a by value. We could accomplish that by the statement

```
Call Add((a), b, c)
```

In this case, rather than passing the reference for the memory location in the calling procedure, a temporary memory location is set up and its reference is passed. Hence, the value of a in the calling program will not be affected by changes that occur in the Sub procedure. The next exercise provides a further illustration of this feature and its behavior.

5.4.1   Hands-on Exercise: Passing by Value or by Reference

STEP 1: In this exercise, we develop a macro that employs passing by value and passing by reference in the same procedure. Start up Excel and open a new workbook called ValRef.xls. Go to the VBE and insert the following module:

```
Sub Test()
x = 1
y = 0
MsgBox "Before Call: x = " & x & " and y = " & y
Call ValRef((x), y)
MsgBox "After Call: x = " & x & " and y = " & y
End Sub
Sub ValRef(x, y)
y = x + 1
x = 0
MsgBox "Within Sub: x = " & x & " and y = " & y
End Sub
```

STEP 2: When you run Sub Test, the first Msgbox shows that x and y have their original assigned values of 1 and 0, respectively:

After the OK button is clicked, the Sub procedure ValRef is called. Notice that (x) is passed by value, whereas y is passed by reference. Inside the Sub, y is assigned the value of x + 1. Since x is equal to 1, y is set equal to 2. Then x is assigned a value of zero. The MsgBox is as follows:

After OK is clicked, control is transferred back to the calling program, where the final MsgBox is displayed:

```
Microsoft Excel                    [×]

       After Call: x = 1 and y = 2

              ┌─────────────┐
              │     OK      │
              └─────────────┘
```

Notice that because x was passed by value, even though it is changed to 0 in the procedure, its original value of 1 is maintained in the main program. The same is not true for y, which was passed by reference.

Another example of passing by value is the passing of an expression to a procedure, as in the statement

```
Call Example(a + 5, b, c)
```

Just as with the constant, the computer first evaluates the expression and places the result in a temporary memory location. The reference for this location is then passed to the procedure. Now it should be clear why the parentheses are used to pass a variable by value. In essence, the parentheses "trick" the computer into thinking that you are passing an expression!

5.5 STATIC VARIABLES

Every time you invoke a procedure, its local variables will be initialized. All numerical variables will be set to zero, and all string variables will be set to a zero-length string (""). On occasion, however, you may not want this to happen. That is, you might want to invoke a procedure several times and have it retain the values of its local variables.

The *Static statement* is designed to define the local variables that you want to retain their values between invocations. A simplified version of the syntax of this statement is

```
Static varname, varname, . . .
```

Here is an example that illustrates how it works:

```
Sub TestStatic()
a = 15
c = Accumulate(a)
MsgBox c
MsgBox Accumulate(28)
End Sub
Function Accumulate(n)
Static sum
sum = sum + n
Accumulate = sum
End Function
```

On the first invocation, a value of 15 is passed to `Accumulate`. Because this is the first time that the function is called, the static variable `sum` has an initial value of 0. Therefore, the addition yields 15. This result is passed back, assigned to c, and displayed as

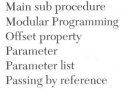

On the second invocation, a value of 28 is passed to `Accumulate`. Because of the Static statement, `sum` has retained its previous value of 15. Therefore, the addition yields a result of 43, which is passed back and displayed as

Microsoft Excel

43

OK

KEY TERMS

Arguments	Main sub procedure	Passing by value
Assign Macro dialogue box	Modular Programming	Procedure
Call statement	Offset property	Static statement
Calling sub procedure	Parameter	Sub procedure
Function procedure	Parameter list	Subroutine
Local variables	Passing by reference	

Problems

1. Modify the Kicker program so that it also computes the product of the hang time and the distance. Use the program to determine, by trial and error, the angle that maximizes the product. Is this a universal result, or is it dependent on the initial velocity? *Challenge questions:* (*a*) Use calculus to confirm your result and its universality. (*b*) How sensitive is the result?

2. Develop a Sub procedure to determine the real roots of the quadratic equation

$$ax^2 + bx + c = 0. \tag{5-5}$$

Recall that the real roots can be determined with the quadratic formula

$$x = \frac{-b \pm \sqrt{b^2 - 4ac}}{2a}. \tag{5-6}$$

In VBA, this formula would be implemented as

```
x1 = (-b + Sqr(b ^ 2 - 4 * a * c)) / (2 * a)
x2 = (-b - Sqr(b ^ 2 - 4 * a * c)) / (2 * a)
```

Test your program for the following cases: a = −1, b = 8, c = 2; and a = 1, b = 4, c = 1. In addition, try a case that yields an imaginary root: a = 7, b = 3, c = 1. What happens?

3. Enter the following labels and values on a new work sheet:

	A	B
1	Before:	
2	a	10
3	b	20
4		
5	After:	
6	a	
7	b	

Develop a Sub procedure to take the values for a and b and switch them. Use a separate Sub procedure to implement the switch.

4. Fill in the values of the variables at each point indicated in the following algorithm:[5]

```
Sub Calc()
i = 7 : j = 5 : k = 8    i        j        k        m        n
                        ____    ____    ____    ____    ____
Call Tester(i, j, k)
                        ____    ____    ____    ____    ____
End Sub
Sub Tester(n, m, i)
Dim j As Integer, k As Integer
                        ____    ____    ____    ____    ____
j = 12
m = j
k = 7
                        ____    ____    ____    ____    ____
End Sub
```

5. Fill in the values of the variables at each point indicated in the following algorithm:

```
Sub Calc()
w = 1 : x = 2 : y = 8    v        w        x        y        z
                        ____    ____    ____    ____    ____
Call Switcheroo(v, (w), x)
                        ____    ____    ____    ____    ____
End Sub
Sub Switcheroo(z, y, x)
                        ____    ____    ____    ____    ____
w = x
x = y
y = w
v = 7
z = z + 3
                        ____    ____    ____    ____    ____
End Sub
```

---

[5] Note that colon delimiters allow you to write multiple statements on a single line. Although this practice is not encouraged, it is useful for cases like the present program, in which we merely want to assign values to a number of variables.

6

Object-oriented Programming

Figure 6.1 shows a simple VBA Sub procedure that fetches two numbers from an Excel worksheet, adds them together, and then displays them back on the worksheet. Notice that the procedure consists of two types of statements:

- **Procedural Programming Statements.** These offer numerical programming functionality (e.g., loops, arrays, logical structures). The simple assignment statement that performs the addition in Figure 6.1 is this type of statement.
- **Object-Oriented Programming (OOP) Statements.** These use phrases such as "Active-Cell.Value" and "Sheets" to perform actions like getting data from the worksheet into a VBA variable or displaying values back on the sheet.

This chapter is designed to afford an insight into *object-oriented programming*, or *OOP*. In particular, its aim is to help you to understand OOP syntax and how it works.

OBJECTIVES

After reading this chapter, you should be able to

- Understand the concept of an object.
- Recognize how methods allow you to manipulate objects.
- Recognize how properties provide information on object attributes.
- Recognize that a collection refers to a group of objects of the same type.
- Use OOP statements to manipulate objects and access their properties.
- Use the With/End With construct to set multiple properties of an object.
- Use OOP statements to transfer data between Excel and VBA.
- Explore OOP by accessing VBAs internal help and documentation.

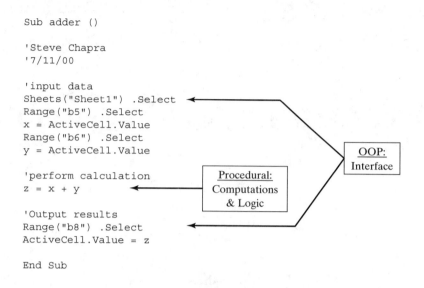

```
Sub adder ()

'Steve Chapra
'7/11/00

'input data
Sheets("Sheet1") .Select
Range("b5") .Select
x = ActiveCell.Value
Range("b6") .Select
y = ActiveCell.Value

'perform calculation
z = x + y

'Output results
Range("b8") .Select
ActiveCell.Value = z

End Sub
```

Figure 6.1. VBA macros consist of procedural and object-oriented programming statements. The former deal with mathematics and logic, whereas the latter provide a means of communicating with and manipulating the Excel interface.

6.1 OBJECTS, PROPERTIES, METHODS, AND COLLECTIONS

Object-oriented programming is based on the notion that software packages can be viewed as consisting of distinct objects with properties that can be manipulated by methods:

- *Object.* A distinct part of a software application.

- *Property.* An attribute of an object.

- *Method.* An action that changes an object's properties or makes the object do something.

An analogy with convenience stores is useful in making these abstract concepts more tangible.[1] Figure 6.2 depicts a trio of convenience store chains: 7-Eleven, Store24, and Speedway. (More can be added to the diagram at will.) These broad umbrella categories are called *applications objects.*

Within an individual application object, such as 7-Eleven, there is a hierarchy of objects. At the highest level are the individual stores in the chain. Each store object in turn consists of a number of objects—the retail area, the parking lot, the rest rooms, etc. Within the retail area are more objects, such as the coolers, the register, and more.

Each of these objects has properties. For example, the coolers have a temperature, a number of shelves, etc. The properties can be adjusted by methods. For instance, a ChangeThermostat method can be invoked to change the cooler's temperature.

---

[1] The idea for this analogy is based on the fast-food analogy from Walkenbach (1999).

Figure 6.2. An object-oriented view of convenience stores.

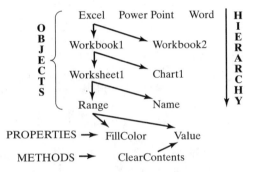

Figure 6.3. An object-oriented view of Microsoft Office.

The same object-oriented perspective can be applied to software. For Microsoft Office, the application objects would be the component programs: Excel, Power Point, Word, etc. Within the Excel object, the top of the object hierarchy would be the open workbooks. Within each workbook, objects would consist of individual worksheets and charts. Worksheets can be broken down further into ranges of cells, names, and so on. (see Figure 6.3.)

As with the convenience stores, each software object has properties. A range object[2] has a value, a fill color, a column, etc. Further, these properties can be adjusted by methods. For instance, a ClearContents method can be invoked to wipe out the values in a range.

The final concept to be mentioned is the *collection*, which is a group of objects of the same type. For example, all the Chart objects in an individual Workbook object are referred to as that Workbook's *Charts*. Similarly, the collection of sheets in a particular Workbook object is called its *Sheets*.

6.1.1   Hands-on Exercise: OOP and a Recorded Macro

Let's record a macro and then interpret the resulting code in light of the previous discussion of OOP.

---

[2] Notice that there is no such thing as a cell object in VBA: A cell is merely a range with a single element. For example, Range("b10") refers to the "range" consisting of the single cell b10.

STEP 1: Open a new workbook, and make sure that the fill color and font color icons are displayed on the menu bar:

Enter the following phrases in cells A1, A2, and B3 (note that the phrase in cell B3 should be italic):

	A	B	C	D	E
1	Engineers				
2	have lots of integrity				
3		*Engineers are creators and builders*			
4					

STEP 2: Making sure that cell B3 is selected, record a macro exactly as outlined in the steps that follows. Begin the recording session by selecting **Tools, <u>M</u>acro, <u>R</u>ecord New Macro**. Name the macro *FormatCell*, and give it the shortcut key *Ctrl–Shift–F*. Make sure that the relative reference button is depressed. Make the text bold and get rid of the italics by depressing the *Italic button* on the menu bar. Set the fill color and font color to yellow and red, respectively, using the buttons on the menu bar. Place the cursor at the boundary between columns B and C, and double-click to broaden the column width so as to encompass the entire phrase. Click on the *Stop Recording button* to terminate the recording session. Place the cursor on cell A1 and press Ctrl–Shift–F. The sheet should now look like this:

	A	B	C
1	**Engineers**		
2	have lots of integrity		
3		**Engineers are creators and builders**	
4			

STEP 3: Move to the VBE with the Alt–F11 shortcut key combination. The following code should be listed[3] in Module1:

```
Sub FormatCell()
'
' FormatCell Macro
' Macro recorded 11/10/2001 by Steven Chapra
'
' Keyboard Shortcut: Ctrl+Shift+F
'
```

---

[3] As in all recording sessions, the code could look different if you did *anything* different than I did.

```
        Selection.Font.Bold = True
        Selection.Font.Italic = False
        With Selection.Interior
            .ColorIndex = 6
            .Pattern = xlSolid
        End With
        Selection.Font.ColorIndex = 3
        ActiveCell.Columns("A:A").EntireColumn.EntireColumn.AutoFit
    End Sub
```

Let's examine this code in light of our previous discussion of OOP. After the documentation comments, the following line was generated when we depressed the *Bold button*:

```
    Selection.Font.Bold = True
```

The object `Selection.Font` refers to the font of the selected cell (in this case, `B3`). The `.Bold` specifies that we are dealing with the object's *Bold property*. By assigning a `True` value to the bold property, we cause the font of the selected cell to be bold. In a similar fashion, the following statement makes the font nonitalic:

```
    Selection.Font.Italic = False
```

Recall that our next move was to set the cell's fill to yellow. As with the font modifications, you would think that the macro recorder would have generated a single line of code. However, in its typical verbose way, the recorder generates additional statements:

```
    With Selection.Interior
        .ColorIndex = 6
        .Pattern = xlSolid
    End With
```

The *With/End With loop* allows you to implement a series of statements applying to a specified object without respecifying the name of the object. The syntax of the statement is

```
    With object
      [statements]
    End With
```

where `object` is the name of the object and `statements` are one or more statements to be executed on the object.

In the current our case, the object is the interior of the selection (`Selection.Interior`). We set its *ColorIndex* property to 6, which represents yellow (Table 6-1). However, in addition, the recorder sets the *Pattern* property to solid. Because the cells originally were solid, this additional statement was unnecessary and could be omitted. Therefore, the following single statement could have been used merely to set the cell's fill color to yellow:

```
    Selection.Interior.ColorIndex = 6
```

TABLE 6-1 Indices for colors in the standard Excel color palette

1. Black	15. Gray (25%)	45. Light Orange
2. White	16. Gray (50%)	46. Orange
3. Red	33. Sky Blue	47. Blue Gray
4. Bright Green	34. Light Turquoise	48. Gray (40%)
5. Blue	35. Light Green	49. Dark Teal
6. Yellow	36. Light Yellow	50. Sea Green
7. Pink	37. Pale Blue	51. Dark Green
8. Turquoise	38. Rose	52. Olive
9. Dark Red	39. Lavender	53. Brown
10. Green	40. Tan	54. Plum
11. Dark Blue	41. Light Blue	55. Indigo
12. Dark Yellow	42. Aqua	56. Gray (80%)
13. Violet	43. Lime	
14. Teal	44. Gold	

The next statement sets the font's *ColorIndex* property to 3, which represents red (Table 6-1):

```
Selection.Font.ColorIndex = 3
```

Finally, the last statement fits the active cell's column width to the width of the widest entry in its column:

```
ActiveCell.Columns("A:A").EntireColumn.EntireColumn.AutoFit
```

When we apply the macro to cell A1, the AutoFit method is applied to column A. That is, the column is widened to fit the widest phrase in the column. Note that this line can also be shortened to

```
ActiveCell.EntireColumn.AutoFit
```

to accomplish the desired effect.

By simplifying as much as possible, the final macro can be reduced to

```
Sub FormatCell()
'
' FormatCell Macro
' Macro recorded 11/10/2001 by Steven Chapra
'
' Keyboard Shortcut: Ctrl+Shift+F
'
    With Selection.Font
        .Bold = True
        .Italic = False
        .ColorIndex = 3
    End With
    Selection.Interior.ColorIndex = 6
    ActiveCell.EntireColumn.AutoFit
End Sub
```

Before moving on, you should recognize that the VBE provides context-sensitive aids that can be very helpful in implementing OOP statements. For example, if you start typing `ActiveCell.` and pause, a drop-down window will appear, listing the object's properties and methods:

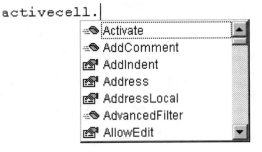

6.2 USING OOP FOR INPUT/OUTPUT

The following statements were used to get a numeric value from a cell on a worksheet "Interface" and then assign the value to the variable `vi`:

```
Sheets("Interface").Select
Range("b10").Select
vi = ActiveCell.Value
```

Let's look at the logic behind these lines. First, we must establish how to select a particular object. To reference a single object within a collection, you type the object's name (enclosed in quotation marks) within parentheses after the name of the collection. For example, the following line would be used to reference the worksheet "Interface":

```
Sheets("Interface")
```

Next, let's reference a range object within this worksheet. The position of an object in an object hierarchy is specified by using a period between the container object. To select a single cell "b10", we would append the range object, as in the following line:

```
Sheets("Interface").Range("b10")
```

Now that we have referenced the cell, we can investigate its properties or act on it by using methods. For example, to select the cell, we must invoke the *Select* method:

```
Sheets("Interface").Range("b10").Select
```

Our knowledge of OOP allows us to interpret this line as specifying that we are selecting the range object "b10" contained in the worksheet object "Interface".

Note that the line of code could be disaggregated by first selecting the sheet and then selecting the range:

```
Sheets("Interface").Select
Range("b10").Select
```

Thus, you can select the sheet once and then select various ranges without repeating the sheet selection.

We can also investigate the properties of the preceding objects. For example, the value of b10 can be represented by

```
Range("b10").Value
```

or, because it is the active cell, by

```
ActiveCell.Value
```

These lines can in turn be used to assign the cell value to a variable. For example,

```
vi = ActiveCell.Value
```

would result in the value of the ActiveCell being assigned to the variable vi.

An example of a method might be one that clears the contents of the ActiveCell. This can be done with

```
ActiveCell.ClearContents
```

After execution of this line, the ActiveCell would be blank.

6.3   LEARNING MORE ABOUT OOP

Aside from other books (for example, Walkenbach, 1999), three vehicles are available for extending your knowledge of OOP:

Recording macros.   As we have shown in this chapter, recording a macro automatically generates corresponding VBA code. Beyond performing the task at hand, this code also provides a way to learn how OOP works.

On-Line Help.   VBA's on-line help provides documentation for every object, property, and method. In VBE, place the cursor anywhere within a keyword, hit the F1 key, and a detailed description containing cross-references and, in some cases, useful examples will appear. For example, the help screen for the Worksheet object is shown in Figure 6.4. If you click Properties or Methods, you will be provided with a complete list of each of these.

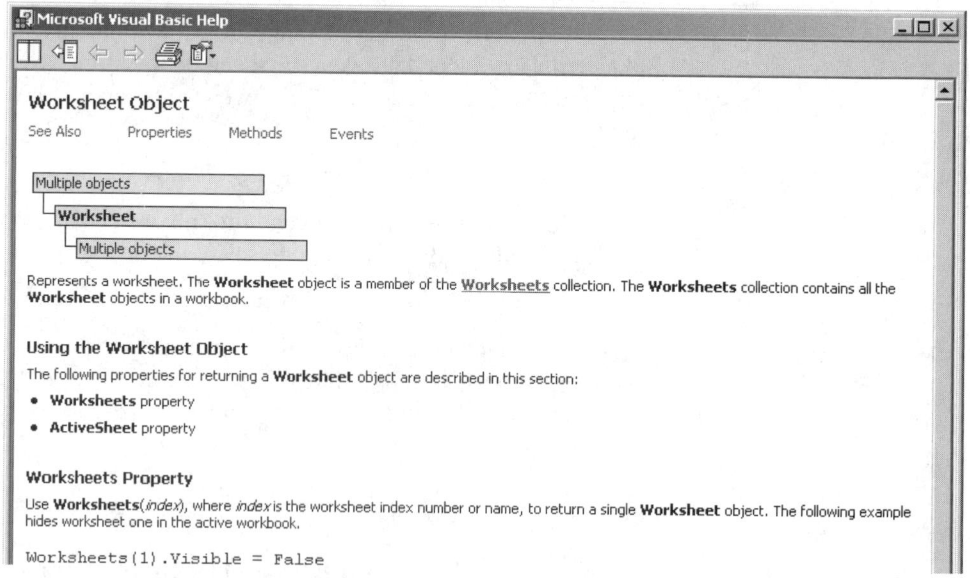

Figure 6.4.   On-line help for the Worksheet object.

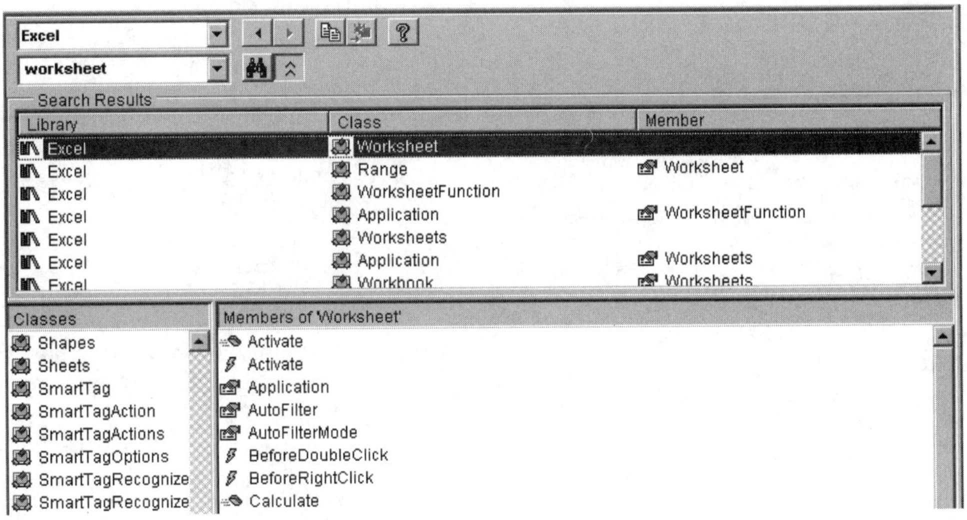

Figure 6.5.   The VBA object browser.

The Object Browser.   This tool allows you to browse through all the available objects. Although it is usually not very useful to beginners, the object browser becomes invaluable to more advanced users. It is invoked in VBE by the menu selection **View, Object Browser** or by hitting the F2 key. The first drop-down list at the top contains all available object libraries. To browse through Excel's objects, select "Excel" from the list. If you want to look through all the objects that deal with worksheets, type "worksheet" in the second drop-down list. The resulting window is shown in Figure 6.5. If you see something that interests you, select it and press the F1 key for details.

KEY TERMS

Applications object	Method	Pattern property
Bold property	Object	Property
Charts	Object Browser	Select
Collection	Object-oriented programming (OOP)	Sheets
ColorIndex property	On-Line Help (F1 key)	With/End With loop

Problems

1. (*a*) Record a relative macro to format a preselected range of cells according to the following specifications:

    - **fill color:** yellow
    - **pattern:** thin reverse diagonal stripes
    - **font:** ArialBlack, blue, bold, and italic
    - **number format:** scientific notation with four decimal places
    - **border:** outline

    (*b*) Develop a Sub procedure that reads a number from a worksheet cell. If the number is below zero, call another Sub to change the cell's format to conform with the specifications from part (*a*). Use your knowledge of OOP to simplify the code as much as possible.

2. (*a*) Open a new workbook and type the following:

```
A3: k      B3: 0.1
A4: w      B4: 1
A6: t      B6: v
A7: 0      B7: = EXP(-$B$3*A7) * COS($B$4*A7)
A8: 1      B8: = EXP(-$B$3*A8) * COS($B$4*A8)
.
.
.
A27: 20   B27: = EXP(-$B$3*A27) * COS($B$4*A27)
```

On Sheet1, use the Chart Wizard to develop an XY plot with data points connected by lines without markers. *Do not format the plot.* At this point, the worksheet should look like Figure 6.6.

Make certain that the cursor is in cell A1, and record a relative macro named Explore with the shortcut key Ctrl–Shift–E. Do the following exactly as specified:

Step 1: Insert a new sheet and rename it "NewSheet."

Step 2: Select "Sheet1."

Step 3: Select "Chart Area" by placing the cursor just inside the upper left-hand corner of the chart (the white area) and clicking once.

Step 4: Repeat Step 3, but select "Plot Area" (by placing the cursor just inside the upper left-hand corner of the plot's gray area)

Step 5: Repeat Step 3, but select the "Legend Box."

Step 6: Double click on the "Chart Title Box." Change the font to 14-point boldface.

Step 7: Select cell A1.

Step 8: Terminate recording.

(*b*) Based on part (*a*), develop a button-triggered Sub procedure that changes the font for the legend box to 16-point boldface italic.

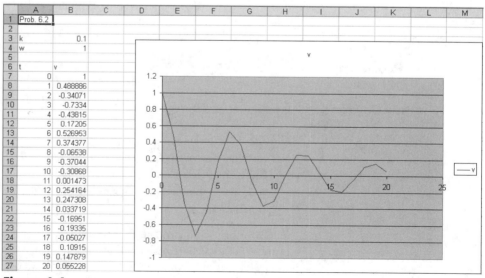

Figure 6.6.

7

Debugging and Testing

Because of mistyping, mathematical errors and logical flaws, you will almost never get a code to work the first time you run it. Many errors or "bugs" will have to be corrected before your program will yield results. Therefore, the first goal of this chapter is to introduce you to tools that can help you obtain a running program.

Furthermore, one of the great misconceptions of novice programmers is that if a program runs, the results it displays must be correct. And God forbid if the results are displayed as colorful plots or animations! In such cases, certain individuals lose any vestige of self-control and will buy anything the computer spits out.

Of course, because we're engineers, we know better. Therefore, the second goal of this chapter is to describe some techniques for testing that your program yields correct results.

SECTIONS

- 7.1 Debugging
- 7.2 The VBA Help Facility
- 7.3 Built-in Debugging Capabilities
- 7.4 Testing

OBJECTIVES

After reading this chapter, you should be able to

- Identify the differences among syntax, run-time and logic errors.
- Navigate around the VBA Help facility.
- Obtain context-sensitive Help by using the F1 key in the VBE.
- Interpret VBA error messages and diagnostics.
- Step through programs and set break points within the VBE.
- Identify the values of variables in break mode.
- Recognize that just because a program runs does not mean that the results are correct.
- Know how testing can be used to verify that a program yields correct results.

7.1   DEBUGGING

A *bug* is an error that prevents your program from performing as expected. The term *debugging* refers to the process of hunting down and correcting these bugs. The bugs come in three major varieties:

- *Syntax errors* violate the rules of the language such as spelling conventions, how numbers are formed, and rules governing the placement of parentheses.[1] Often, syntax errors are the result of simple mistakes, such as typing `Activr-Cell.Value` rather than `ActiveCell.Value`. A syntax error is detected when you attempt to run your macro. The computer displays an error message, called a *diagnostic* because the computer is helping you to diagnose the problem.

- *Execution errors* are errors that occur when a syntax-error-free program runs. They are sometimes referred to as *run-time errors*. An execution error results when a statement attempts an invalid operation, such as division by zero. In that case, an error message will be displayed.

- *Logic errors*, as the name implies, are due to faulty program logic. These errors are usually the worst type, because no diagnostics will appear. At best, your program will produce obviously absurd results; at worst, your program will appear to be working properly, in the sense that it executes and generates results, but the output will be incorrect.

The chapter includes an introduction to some of the debugging tools that are available in VBA. Also covered are methods for testing to ensure that your program yields correct results.

7.2   THE VBA HELP FACILITY

VBA has a built-in help facility that is valuable both as a learning tool and as a source of information that is useful in understanding and correcting errors. Help is invoked in three primary ways:

- By using the Help menu selection

- With the F1 hot key

- As the result of an error message

7.2.1   Help Menu

As with all Microsoft Office applications, VBA offers help to the user. Once the Help option is invoked (through the menu or via the F1 hot key), the Help dialogue box appears (Figure 7.1). Notice that there are three tabs. Of the three, I find the Index and Contents tabs the most useful.

---

[1] Here is a tip: A nice way to pick up syntax errors immediately is to type all statements in lowercase. Then, when you hit the return key, the first letter of all keywords should automatically be capitalized (and colored blue). If this does not occur, you know that you have made a mistake.

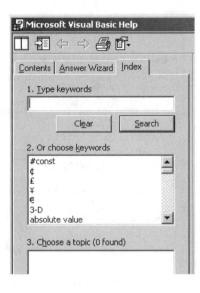

Figure 7.1.   The VBA Help dialogue box.

The *Index tab* provides descriptions of VBA keywords. It is used when you know or have an idea of the name of a keyword, but do not understand its purpose or use. For example, suppose that you forget how the Function statement works. You would start entering the word "function" in the *1. Type keyword* slot. As you type, matches will appear in the *2. Or choose keywords* slot. When you get far enough, "function" will appear. Double–click on it, and a description will be displayed, giving you all the gory details:

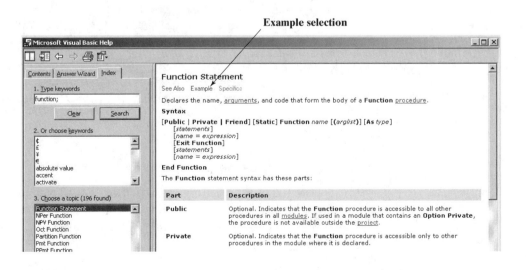

Beyond the basic description, I find the Example selection particularly useful. In this case, selecting Example yields the following display:

Function Statement Example

This example uses the **Function** statement to declare the name, arguments, and code that form the body of a **Function** procedure. The last example uses hard-typed, initialized **Optional** arguments.

```
' The following user-defined function returns the square root of the
' argument passed to it.
Function CalculateSquareRoot(NumberArg As Double) As Double
    If NumberArg < 0 Then      ' Evaluate argument.
        Exit Function     ' Exit to calling procedure.
    Else
        CalculateSquareRoot = Sqr(NumberArg)     ' Return square root.
    End If
End Function
```

Thus, VBA Help displays examples to show you how the Function statement is implemented. Beyond learning about Function, these examples are often quite useful in their own right and can provide great ideas on other aspects of the language.

The *Contents tab* is like an automated users' manual. When you first select it, a table of contents is displayed. Then, by clicking on various selections, you can work your way down to the particular information you require. For example, suppose that you forget how the message box function works. Then contents can be queried to yield the following display:

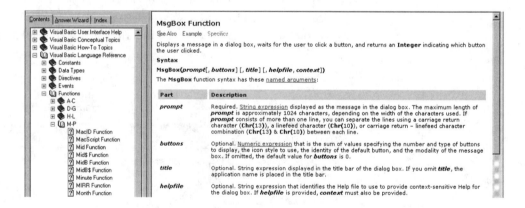

7.2.2   Context-Sensitive Help and the F1 Key

Suppose you want to learn more about the *InputBox* function. An alternative to going through the Help tabs is to type the keyword in the VBE window. With your cursor anywhere on the word, press F1. Help will automatically open up to the entry describing the *InputBox* function:

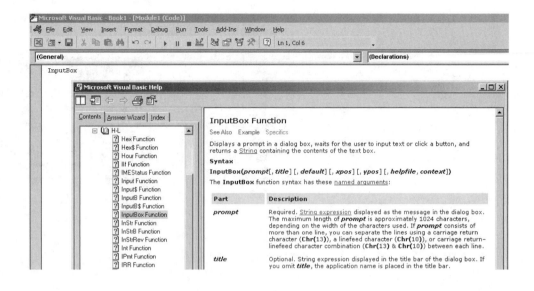

7.2.3 Accessing Help from Error Messages

Sometimes VBA will display a dialogue box to alert you that an error has occurred. Sometimes the dialogue box will have a Help button displayed. In such cases, clicking the button will display a description of the error.

7.3 BUILT-IN DEBUGGING CAPABILITIES

The most straightforward debugging technique consists of *closely examining your code to see whether you can locate the problem.* If you're lucky, the error might jump right out, and you can quickly correct it.

7.3.1 Passive Debugging: VBA Error Messages

Beyond scrutinizing your code, you can utilize VBA's built-in error detection features. For example, we deliberately included a syntax error in the following code (instead of a minus sign, we typed an underscore in the equation):

```
Sub Example()
a = 5 _ 3
End Sub
```

When this code is run, the program displays an error message box informing you that an "Invalid character was used." The place where the error occurred is highlighted, and the line's color is changed to red:

```
Sub Example()
a = 5 ▋ 3
End Sub
```

Microsoft Visual Basic ✕

⚠ Compile error:

Invalid character

OK   Help

Another example involves division by zero:

```
Sub Example()
a = 5
b = 0
c = a / b
End Sub
```

When this code is run, something a little different happens: An error message appears, informing you that you have committed a run-time error involving division by zero. The error message box looks like the following:

```
Sub Example()
a = 5
b = 0
c = a / b
End Sub
```

Microsoft Visual Basic

Run-time error '11':

Division by zero

Continue   End   Debug   Help

The box displays three buttons: End, Debug, and Help. The *End button* merely terminates the program.

The *Debug button* interrupts program execution and puts you into *break mode*. In the present case, you are transferred back into the code window, where the line containing the error will be highlighted:

```
Sub Example()
a = 5
b = 0
⇨  c = a / b
End Sub
```

If you move the mouse pointer carefully over the variable b in the division formula, a nice result occurs. The variable's value will be displayed in a small pop-up window as follows:

```
Sub Example()
a = 5
b = 0
⇨  c = a / b
End Sub b=0
```

Move the mouse pointer over to a to view its value. This can be very helpful in finding errors in more complicated formulas (for example, errors in which numerous divisions occur).

Pressing the *Help button* would have resulted in VBA displaying an explanation of the error:

Division by zero (Error 11)

Specifics

Division by zero isn't possible. This error has the following cause and solution:

* The value of an <u>expression</u> being used as a divisor is zero.

    Check the spelling of <u>variables</u> in the expression. A misspelled variable name can implicitly create a numeric variable that is initialized to zero. Check previous operations on variables in the expression, especially those passed into the <u>procedure</u> as <u>arguments</u> from other procedures.

For additional information, select the item in question and press F1 (in Windows) or HELP (on the Macintosh).

Although the meaning of this error is quite obvious, in other cases the help facility might assist you in figuring out an otherwise obscure error.

Note that after you correct the error, you would want to run the program again to make certain that everything is fixed. Before you can do that, however, you must get out of break mode by clicking on the *reset button* at the top of the editor window: ■

7.3.2 Active Debugging

A common problem in many programs involves one or more variables that fail to take on the values you expect. In such cases, a helpful debugging technique is to monitor the variable or variables while your code runs. The easiest way to do this consists of inserting temporary MsgBox functions in your routine to display values as the program proceeds. Still, VBA also offers more powerful means of tracking variables. The next hands-on exercise explores some of these facilities.

7.3.3 Hands-on Exercise: The VBA Debugger

STEP 1: Start up Excel and type the following entries into Sheet1:

A1: Sphere Program
A2: Your Name
A5: radius   B5: 2   C5: m
A7: area   C7: m^2
A8: volume   C8: m^3

Save these entries as a file named sphere.xls.

STEP 2: Switch over to the Visual Basic Editor, insert a new module, and type in the following sub procedure?

```
Sub Sphere()
pii = 3.14159
'Get value of Radius from user
Sheets("Sheet1").Select
Range("b5").Select
radius = ActiveCell.Value
' Compute volume
volume = 4 / 3 * pii * radius ^ 3
' Compute surface area
area = 4 * pii * radius ^ 2
' Display results
Range("b7:b8").ClearContents
Range("b7").Select
ActiveCell.Value = area
ActiveCell.Offset(1, 0).Select
ActiveCell.Value = volume
Range("b5").Select
End Sub
```

STEP 3: Back in Excel, create a button that the user can click on to trigger the macro. The resulting sheet should look like this:

	A	B	C	D	E
1	Sphere Program				
2	Ima N. Gineer			Run	
3					
4					
5	radius	2	m		
6					
7	area	50.2654	m^2		
8	volume	33.5103	m^3		

STEP 4: Now let's return to the VBA editor and explore some of its debugging tools. As described previously, displaying a message box essentially halts your code in midexecution, and clicking the **OK** button resumes execution. Another way to find errors is to step through your program—that is, execute it line by line and take a look at the values of variables at each step along the way. To do this, press the F8 key. Notice that the first line of the program is highlighted in yellow and that a yellow arrow appears in the gray margin to the left of your code.

Now press the F8 key again. The highlight should jump to the second executable line in the program. Evidently, you are stepping through the program.

Next, press F8 five more times, so that the line in which the area is calculated is highlighted in yellow. Move the mouse pointer carefully over the variable "radius" in the volume formula. The value of this variable will be displayed in a small pop-up window as shown in the following display:

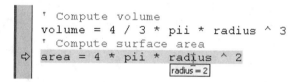

Move the mouse pointer over to "pii" and "volume", and you can see their values, too.

At this point, you could keep hitting F8 until you stepped to the end of the program. Since this would be extremely inconvenient in a long program, however, an alternative is to hit the reset button at the top of the editor window to stop the stepping-through process.

STEP 5: Because stepping through the program might not be the best approach for finding bugs in a long program, wouldn't it be nice if you could halt the execution of the program at a particular location, look at the values of some variables, and then proceed on your way? Well, that's exactly what setting a *breakpoint* can do for you.

To set a breakpoint in your code, move the cursor to the line at which you want execution to stop and press F9, or just click on the gray margin to the left of the statement. Try this for the area statement. As the following display shows, VBA both highlights the line to remind you that you have set a breakpoint there and inserts a large dot in the margin.

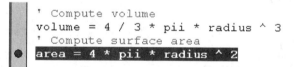

When you execute the procedure (for example, by hitting the *Run Sub UserForm* button in the VBA tool bar ▶), VBA goes into *Break mode* when the line with the breakpoint is located. (Try it). In break mode, the word [break] is displayed on the VBA title bar. Notice how the program has executed down to the breakpoint and is in "suspended animation." You can move the cursor up to previous lines to check the values of various variables at this point. To get out of break mode and resume program execution, press F5 or click the *Run Sub UserForm* button.

To remove a breakpoint, click the large dot in the gray margin, or move the cursor to the highlighted line and press F9. Note that you can set up multiple breakpoints in a code. To remove all breakpoints in a module, press Ctrl–Shift–F9.

7.4 TESTING

One of the great misconceptions of the novice programmer is the belief that if a program runs and prints out results, it is correct. Of particular danger are results that appear to be "reasonable," but are in fact wrong. Consequently, before you use your program to make engineering decisions, you should perform a series of tests to make certain that it is correct. The following suggestions will aid you in testing:

- If possible, generate the correct answer with your calculator or Excel itself. Then compare that answer with the result obtained by your program for the same input data.
- Subject your program to a wide variety of test cases, including the following:

  - a range of typical inputs. (For example, for the quadratic equation, you could input coefficients that will create real, complex, and single roots.)
  - unusual, but valid, data. (For example, for the quadratic equation, you could input all zero coefficients.)
  - incorrect data to test the program's error-handling capabilities. (For example, you could input a negative value for a parameter (such as mass) that cannot be negative.)

- Have other individuals run your program and try to crash it. This is called a *beta test* and is a great way to find errors.

In very large and complicated codes, you might not uncover every error. However, if you carefully subject your program to tests like the ones just outlined, you will go a long way towards making a more reliable, more robust product.

KEY TERMS

Beta test	Debug button	Execution errors	Logic errors
Break mode	Debugging	Help button	Reset button
Bug	Diagnostic	Index tab	Run-time errors
Contents tab	End button	InputBox function	Syntax errors

Problems

1. Use the quadratic formula to solve for the roots of

    (a) $x^2 - 5x + 2 = 0$

    (b) $5x - 3 = 0$

    (c) $x^2 - 2x + 3 = 0$

   The following VBA procedure performs the same calculation. Enter it into the VBE.

```
Sub Quadroots ()
MsgBox "Enter coefficients for quadratic: a*x^2 + b*x + c"
a = InputBox ("a = ")
b = InputBox ("b = ")
c = InputBox ("c = ")
'quadratic formula
d = b ^ 2 - 4 * a * c
r1 = (-b + d ^ 0.5) / (2 * a)
r2 = (-b - d ^ 0.5) / (2 * a)
MsgBox "r1 = " & r1 & " and r2 = " & r2
End Sub
```

Debug the program so that it yields the correct result for case (*a*). When you apply the program to cases (*b*) and (*c*), what errors messages does VBA display? What mathematical problems actually caused the errors?

2. Enter the following code into VBA and add breakpoints as shown

```
Sub ForNext()
For i = 8 To -4 Step -5
   'body of loop
Next i
'after the loop
End Sub
```

Run the program and record the value of i as each breakpoint is reached. Describe how the loop operates in light of your results.

8

Data Typing and Variable Scope

Engineers primarily use computers to manipulate numbers (integer and decimal values). However, beyond our interest in numbers, we must also deal with other forms of information. Examples include alphanumeric (names, dates, etc.) and logical (true or false) data. Each of these data types is stored within different types of memory location within the computer.

VBA has two ways of dealing with data types. First, VBA can automatically decide the type of each piece of information. Alternatively, you can explicitly specify the types yourself. Because it requires less effort, the former would seem preferable. However, there are two reasons why the latter approach is superior: your macros will run more efficiently and will be easier to debug. This chapter will describe these benefits along with reviewing VBA's capabilities for controlling which modules and procedures have access to particular variables.

SECTIONS

- 8.1   Data Types
- 8.2   Type Declaration
- 8.3   Variable Scope and Lifetime

OBJECTIVES

After reading this chapter, you should be able to

- Differentiate among the principle data types used by engineers: numeric, string and logical.
- Understand that the choice of numeric types depends on calculation requirements, memory and speed.
- Understand the Variant type and how it works.
- Define variable type with the Dim statement.
- Understand the benefits of variable typing and the Option Explicit statement.
- Understand when the Const statement is appropriate.
- Understand the concepts of variable scope and lifetime.
- Recognize how the Public statements makes variables globally available in a project.

8.1   DATA TYPES

Suppose that we assign a simple integer constant to a variable by means of the statement

```
n = 3
```

As illustrated in Figure 8.1, the assignment statement results in the storage of the value (3) in a computer memory location that is referenced by a variable name (n).

VBA allows you store many other types of information beyond that associated with simple integers. In this chapter, we limit ourselves to the following types of information most commonly used by engineers:[1]

- Numbers

    - Integer (or whole) numbers (Integer and Long)
    - Real (or decimal) numbers (Single or Double)

- Characters (String)
- Logical (Boolean)

From Figure 8.1, we see that each of these types of information requires different types of memory locations (as suggested by the different sizes of the mailboxes). This fact has serious implications for the speed and memory requirements of our macro programs.

8.1.1   Numeric Information

VBA allows you to work with two major categories of numbers: integer and real. Each of these categories is in turn divided into two further types. The general picture is as follows:

Integers. The integers are whole numbers that are used for counting. They come in two types:

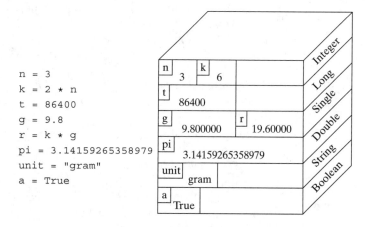

Figure 8.1.   Illustration of how different variable types are stored in the computer's memory.

---

[1] For those who are curious, the VBA help facility provides the means of learning more about other data types, such as Date, Byte, Currency, Decimal, and Object.

- *Integer type.* These are whole numbers such as 6256 and −37. Because they are stored in a memory location consisting of 2 bytes,[2] they range from −32,768 to 32,767.
- *Long type.* These are used for whole numbers that exceed the range of the Integer type. They are stored in 4 bytes and range from −2,147,483,648 to 2,147,483,647.

Real. In general, the real types are decimal numbers used for measuring. They are sometimes referred to as *floating-point numbers.* As with the integers, they come in two (sub)types:

- *Single type.* Examples are 3.14159 and −9.81. These are stored in 4 bytes (32 bits). One bit is used for the sign, 8 for the exponent, and 23 for the mantissa. A real number of type single represents about 7 significant digits of precision and ranges from -3.402823×10^{38} to $-1.401298 \times 10^{-45}$ for negative values and from 1.401298×10^{-45} to 3.402823×10^{38} for positive values. This is more than enough precision and range for most engineering and scientific calculations.
- *Double type.* These are used for real numbers for which more precision is required. A real number of type double is stored in 8 bytes and represents about 15 significant digits. Such a number ranges from $-1.79769313486231 \times 10^{308}$ to $-4.94065645841247 \times 10^{-324}$ for negative values and from $4.94065645841247 \times 10^{-324}$ to $1.79769313486232 \times 10^{308}$ for positive values.

For Single and Double types, *scientific numbers* are represented in *E notation*—that is,

$$m \times 10^e \rightarrow mEe$$

where m is the *mantissa* and e is the *exponent* of the number. For example, the number 1×10^{-5} is represented as `1E-5`. Note that if the sign of the exponent is positive, it does not have to be included in the representation of the number. Thus, `6.022E+23` and `6.022E23` are equivalent.

You might wonder why there are so many options. Basically, it boils down to the trade-off between calculation, memory, and processing-time requirements:

Calculation Requirements.   Although the Integer and Single types are adequate for many computations, some require the larger magnitude and precision of the Long and Double types. For example, suppose that you want to use a variable to contain the value of the number of seconds after midnight. Because the number ranges from 0 to 86,400 (60 × 60 × 24), you would exceed the range of the Integer type (−32,768 through 32,767) and would require a Long integer. Similarly, at times, you might need to represent decimal numbers with a high degree of precision. For instance, you might have to perform millions of additions and subtractions in a sequential calculation. In certain cases, round-off errors can accumulate. Using double-precision variables can sometimes mitigate the effects of such errors.

Memory Requirements.   A price is paid for using more bytes to represent numbers. That is, using more bytes requires more computer memory. Therefore, from a memory

---

[2] A *byte* consists of 8 *bits* (short for *binary digits*). A detailed description of how bytes and bits are used to store numbers can be found in Chapra and Canale (1994, 2001).

perspective, Integer and Single are preferable to Long and Double types because the former require less memory. Of course, nowadays computers have more than enough memory for routine engineering computations. Still, in more advanced contexts, memory limitations can be very important.

Processing-Time Requirements. You might presume that because they hold more information, the Long and Double types would require more processing time than Integer and Single. Although that is the conventional wisdom, it is not necessarily true for VBA. In particular, VBA processes double-precision numbers more efficiently than single-precision numbers. We will explore this point at the end of section 8.2.

8.1.2   Character, or "String," Information

Character, or alphanumeric, information refers to sequences of characters, called *String type* in VBA. A string can include letters, numbers, spaces, and punctuation. Examples are names and dates, such as "Sarah Jones" and "Oct. 1, 1998".

VBA allows variable-length and fixed-length strings. *Variable-length strings* are used when the number of characters is unknown. In contrast, *fixed-length strings* are employed when the number of characters, or at least their upper limit, is known (as with phone or credit-card numbers). A variable-length string can contain up to approximately 2 billion ($2^{31} = 2,147,483,648$) characters.[3] A fixed-length string can contain 1 to approximately 64K ($2^{16} = 65,536$) characters.[4]

Note that numeric codes are what is actually used to represent the letters and symbols in computer memory. In particular, the letters of the alphabet are numbered in ascending order. This is the basis for VBA's capability of sorting strings in alphabetical order.

8.1.3   Logical, or "Boolean," Information

Called *Boolean type* in VBA, logical constants and variables can take on only two values: True or False. An example of how type Boolean is used is illustrated by the following Sub procedure:

```
Sub BoolDemo()
a = InputBox("What is the answer (True or False)?")
If a Then
  MsgBox "The answer is true"
Else
  MsgBox "The answer is false"
End If
End Sub
```

If you enter `True` into `InputBox`, it will be stored in variable a. Then the `If` statement will be true, and the message box will display "The answer is true". If you enter `False`, "The answer is false" will appear.

---

[3] Talk about "overkill"!
[4] Ditto!

8.2   TYPE DECLARATION

Performing a *type declaration* refers to specifying the type of each variable explicitly. Although declaring variable types is mandatory in some computer languages, it is voluntary in VBA. In fact, if you don't declare the variable type, VBA employs a special variable type for the purpose: Variant.

8.2.1   Variant Data Type

The *Variant type* is like a chameleon. In other words, the computer chooses the type for you, depending on the context. For example, if you were dealing with whole numbers in the range from −32,768 to 32,767, the computer would opt for the Integer type. However, if you used a number like 86,400, VBA would automatically select the Long type. If you include a decimal, VBA sets the number to Double.[5]

The *VarType function* provides a useful tool for determining the type of a variable. Its syntax is

```
VarType(varname)
```

where *varname* is the variable in question. The function returns a numeric code indicating the variable type. The codes for the commonly used types are as follows:

Value	Type
2	Integer
3	Long
4	Single
5	Double
8	String
11	Boolean

Let's use the VarType function to explore how VBA changes the variable type, depending on the context. The following code illustrates how this works:

```
Sub BoolDemo()
x = 32767
MsgBox VarType(x)
x = 32768
MsgBox VarType(x)
x = 3.14159
MsgBox VarType(x)
x = "Ima Student"
MsgBox VarType(x)
x = True
MsgBox VarType(x)
End Sub
```

When this code is run, the values 2, 3, 5, 8, and 11 will be displayed. In other words, the variable x changes type from Integer to Long to Double to String to Boolean. Recall

---

[5] This is probably because Excel itself uses double precision by default.

that because an Integer variable uses 2 bytes, it can hold values up to and including 32,767. Larger whole numbers must be stored as Long numbers. Because the first value assigned is equal to a whole number (32,767), the variable x initially takes on the Integer type (VarType = 2). When we subsequently assign the whole number 32,768, x switches to the Long type (VarType = 3). When we assign a decimal number (3.14159) to x, it changes to Double (VarType = 5). When the program senses the quotation marks in the next assignment statement, it changes x to the String type. Finally, when the program recognizes that a True value is being assigned, x becomes Boolean.

At this point, you might be saying, "What a deal. I don't have to think!" Unfortunately, you pay a price for letting VBA do the thinking for you, because it takes time for VBA to make the decisions. In contrast, if you explicitly declare the type of each variable, you will gain two major benefits:

- *Your macros will run faster and use less memory.* As just mentioned, every time VBA runs into a Variant type, it must stop and "think" in order to decide which type of storage location it requires. If it "knows" the data type, it doesn't have to make this decision and hence allocates only the necessary memory.
- *You will avoid problems with misspelled variable names.* Suppose that you use an undeclared variable name, such as mass. Somewhere in your macro, you could misspell it in an assignment statement, say,

```
mas = 68.1
```

Such misspellings are difficult to spot and will usually not trigger an error message. Thus, unbeknownst to you, a serious error could result. However, if you explicitly declare your variable types, the computer would display a message to alert you that a compile error has occurred:

8.2.2 The Dim Statement

Now that we've established the importance of data typing, how do you do it? Although there are several possible ways, the *Dim* (short for *Dim*ension) *statement* provides the most straightforward approach. In its simplest manifestation, it has the general syntax

```
Dim varname [As type], varname [As type], . . .
```

where *varname* is the variable name and *type* is the variable's data type.

It is a good practice to place all your Dim statements at the beginning of each procedure. In addition, it's not a bad idea to group them by type. For example, the start of a program might look something like this:

```
Option Explicit

Sub Example()

Dim i As Integer, n As Integer
Dim tseconds As Long
Dim x As Single, v As Single
Dim z As Double
Dim phrase as String
Dim SSNumber As String * 9
Dim response As Boolean
        .
        .
        .
```

Suppose that you then wrote the statement

```
i = "October 1, 1998"
```

Compilation of this statement would result in an error message, because you're telling the computer to put a "square peg in a round hole"; that is, you're telling it to store a string constant in an integer memory location. If you do that, the program will not execute and you'll get an error message.

The type specification for a fixed-length string is written as `String * n`, where n is the number of characters. For example, the statement

```
Dim SSNumber As String * 11
```

allows you to store nine-digit U.S. social security numbers along with the two delimiting dashes, as in

```
SSnumber = "016-56-7782"
```

Notice that each variable has to be declared individually. People who have been trained in other languages, such as Fortran, often make the mistake that a Single type declaration can be made at the end of each Dim statement, as in

```
Dim x, v As Single
```

In this case, only v would be single precision. VBA will assume that x has not been given a type and will automatically make it a Variant.

8.2.3   Option Explicit

Although not declaring variable types is usually no problem in small programs, *I strongly, strongly recommend that you define the type of all variables.* In all of my programs, I force the issue by placing the following line at the beginning of each of my modules:

```
Option Explicit
```

If such a line is included, variable typing is mandatory.

I feel so strongly about this point that I ensure that the Option Explicit statement is automatically inserted in each new module I create by checking the *Require Variable Declaration box* in the editor tab of the Options dialogue box (you get there by the VBE menu selections **Tools, Options**):

Thereafter, the Option Explicit statement will be automatically included at the start of each new module.

8.2.4 Hands-on Exercise: Run Time for Single and Double Precision

Before proceeding, let's explore the time benefit that is gained by declaring variables. Our examination will also provide some insight into the peculiarities of VBA's processing of single- and double-precision numbers.

STEP 1: Open up an Excel workbook, insert a module, and enter the following Sub procedure:

```
Sub Test()
x = 1
dx = 1.00001
Time1 = Timer
For i = 1 To 20000000
  x = Sin(x * dx)
Next i
Time2 = Timer
Runtime = Time2 - Time1
MsgBox Runtime
End Sub
```

This code uses a For/Next loop to perform 20 million evaluations of the sine of the product of two numbers. Notice that no type declaration is included. The *Timer function* returns a value (of type Single) representing the number of seconds elapsed since midnight. Thus, the program will display its own run time, in seconds. My computer (a 1.5-GHz Pentium 4) took about 9.7 s to perform the 20 million evaluations. Run the module on your own computer and record the run time.

STEP 2: Change the beginning of your program to include Option Explicit, and declare the variables as shown:

```
Option Explicit
Sub Test()
Dim i As Long
Dim x As Double, dx As Double
Dim Time2 As Single, Time1 As Single, Runtime As Single
x = 1
    .
    .
    .
```

Notice that we have declared the two variables that are involved in the computation (x and dx) as Double. This is what would have occurred anyway if they had not been declared or had been declared Variant. Because it goes well above 32,767, the variable i is typed as Long. On my computer, the resulting run time for this version of the program was 4.6 s. Thus, because we declared the variable types, the run time was reduced approximately in half.

STEP 3: Finally, declare x and dx as Single:

```
Dim x As Single, dx As Single
```

The resulting run time in this case was 5.7 s. This time is better than that of the nondeclaration scenario of Step 1, but is somewhat slower than the double-precision case. This result is counterintuitive, in that we would expect the single-precision case to be faster because the computer is manipulating smaller packets of information.

There are a number of possible explanations for the slower runtime of the single-precision case. It might mean that Microsoft spent a lot more time on the internal coding for double precision than for single precision. In fact, Microsoft may be borrowing some routines that have been optimized for the spreadsheet side of Excel, where everything is double precision. Also, it's possible that the double-precision code takes direct advantage of the floating-point numerical processor part of the Pentium chip, whereas the single precision code does not.

8.2.5 Type Declaration Characters

In "olde-style" Basic, variables and constants could be typed by appending a special type declaration character. The type declaration characters are as follows:[6]

Type	Suffix
Integer	%
Long	&
Single	!
Double	#
String	$

Here's how the characters work: Suppose that you enter the statement

```
a = 3
```

---

[6] The Boolean type does not have a suffix.

If a has not previously been typed, VBA would automatically make it an Integer type. Suppose that you wanted a to be a Long type. One way to override such automatic assignment would be to rewrite the statement as

```
a& = 3
```

Because of the appended ampersand, VBA recognizes that `a&` is a Long variable and stores it accordingly.

Although I don't recommend using suffixes, it is nice to know about them. For example, if you type a whole number with a decimal point, say, b = 7., and hit enter, the VBA compiler will automatically append a pound sign:

```
b = 7#
```

This is just VBA's way of telling you that it automatically sets decimal constants to the Double type.

8.2.6 The Const Statement

There are certain variables that you never want to change, such as mathematical or physical constants. Examples are π, Avogadro's number, and the gravitational constant. VBA provides the *Const* statement for such variables:

```
Const constname [As type] = value
```

Beyond its function of specifying that the variable is a constant,[7] the Const statement also provides a means of assigning the type of the constant. The following statements are illustrative:

```
Const pi As Double = 3.14159265358979
Const g As Double = 9.81, Avog As Double = 6.022E+23
```

After a constant is declared, it cannot be modified or assigned a new value.

8.3   VARIABLE SCOPE AND LIFETIME

Figure 8.2 shows how procedures and modules are organized within an Excel Workbook. A key question related to the scheme's effective operation is how to control the flow of information among each of the elements.

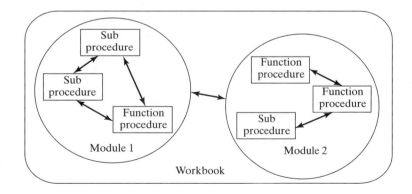

Figure 8.2.   Illustration of how procedures and modules are organized within an Excel Workbook. The arrows indicate the direction of the flow of information among the various elements.

---

[7] Note that, although the statement "the variable is a constant" sounds contradictory, it really isn't. What it says is that a computer variable takes on the value of one, and only one, number, which makes perfectly good sense. If we were talking purely mathematics, the statement "the (mathematical) variable is a (mathematical) constant" would be a contradiction.

The term *variable scope* refers to which procedures have access to what information during a program's execution. A related concept, *variable lifetime*, refers to when a variable's memory location is created and when it is wiped clean.

8.3.1 The Parameter List

One way to control a variable's scope is via a procedure's parameter, or argument, list. Let's review this topic in light of type declaration. The procedures that follow were written within a single module. The first procedure sends two variables to another procedure that switches their values:

```
Option Explicit
Sub Scope()
Dim x As Integer, y As Integer
x = 6
y = 8
Call Switch(x, y)
MsgBox x
MsgBox y
End Sub

Sub Switch(a, b)
Dim d As Integer
d = a
a = b
b = d
End Sub
```

Because we have included an `Option Explicit` statement at the beginning of the module, variable type declaration must be used in both procedures. Thus, the variables x and y must be dimensioned in Sub Scope. This results in two memory locations being established to hold their values. Thus begins the *lifetime* of these two variables.

Next, x and y are passed to Sub Switch via the argument list and are assigned to the variables a and b. When a variable name is passed to a procedure via an argument, no new memory location is created. Rather, the computer will reference the original memory locations in Sub Scope in order to obtain the values of the variables. As a consequence, because memory locations have already been set up for x and y, a and b do not have to be dimensioned in Sub Switch. They merely serve as temporary names that can be used to access the values of x and y within that Sub procedure.

In contrast, the variable d must be dimensioned. It is called a *local variable*, because it exists only within Sub Switch. When that procedure is invoked, a memory location is set up to hold values for d. Once the `End Sub` statement is reached, VBA wipes out the memory location. Hence, the lifetime of d spans only the period when Sub Switch is active. That's why the values of all local variables are initialized each time a Sub procedure is invoked. All numerical variables will be set to zero, and all string variables will be set to a zero-length string (""").

After we return to the main procedure, the variables x and y are still "alive and well." Only after Sub Scope's `End Sub` statement is reached will their lifetimes end. (That is, their memory locations will be destroyed.)

Note that *Static* variables are a special case. For example, the variable d could have been declared with the statement

```
Static d as Integer
```

This declaration would cause the memory location for d to stay "alive" after Sub Switch is finished. If the procedure is called again, the variable will still hold its old value.

8.3.2 Scope and Declaration

Like the parameter list, type declaration can be used to control a variable's scope. As shown in Figure 8.3, this can be done at the procedure, module, and workbook levels:

- *Procedure variables* are declared within a procedure and can be accessed only by that procedure. They are created when the procedure starts, and they are destroyed when the procedure terminates.
- *Module variables* are declared at the beginning of a module (before the first procedure in the module). They can be accessed by all procedures within the module. They are created when the module starts, and they stay in existence until the module terminates.
- *Workbook* (or *global*) *variables* can be accessed by all procedures in all modules. They are declared by placing a *Public statement* before the first procedure in a module.

A simple representation of the Public statement's syntax is

```
Public varname [As type],...
```

where `varname` is the variable's name and `type` denotes the variable's data type. Note that the Public keyword can be combined with the Const statement to make constants global:

```
Public Const constname As type = expression
```

An example of such a combination is the definition of mathematical constants like π, which might be needed in several different modules:

```
Public Const pi As Double = 3.14159265358979
```

An example of declaring a variable at the module level is provided by the following code, which is equivalent to the Sub Scope and Switch procedures described in Sec. 8.3.1:

```
Option Explicit

Dim x As Integer, y As Integer
Sub Scope()
```

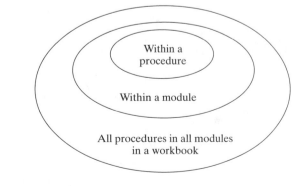

Figure 8.3. Illustration of the different levels of variable scope.

```
x = 6
y = 8
Call Switch
MsgBox x
MsgBox y
End Sub

Sub Switch()
Dim d As Integer
d = x
x = y
y = d
End Sub
```

Notice that we have moved the Dim statement for x and y before the first Sub procedure. Consequently, the memory locations of x and y are available in both Sub procedures. Hence, they do not have to be passed via the argument list, so that the Switch routine is no longer written in terms of a and b. However, the local variable d must still be dimensioned in Sub Switch.

KEY TERMS

Boolean type	Lifetime	String type
Const statement	Local variable	Timer function
Dim statement	Long type numbers	Type declaration
Double type numbers	Option Explicit	Variable lifetime
E notation	Public statement	Variable scope
Fixed-length strings	Require Variable Declaration box	Variable-length strings
Floating-point numbers	Scientific numbers	Variant type
Global variable	Single type numbers	VarType function
Integer type numbers	Static variable	

Problems

1. Boltzmann's constant is equal to 11.7×10^{-8} cal/(cm^2 d K^4). Write a VBA statement to assign the value of Boltzmann's constant in scientific notation to a variable sigma.

2. Fill in the values of the variables at each point indicated in the following algorithm:

```
Option Explicit
Dim a As Integer
Sub Calc()
Dim b As Integer
Dim c As Integer
Dim d As Integer
Dim e As Single
a = -1 : b = 2.1 : c = 8 : d = 4
```

a	b	c	d	e
_____	_____	_____	_____	_____

```
Call Switch(b, c, d)
```

a	b	c	d	e
_____	_____	_____	_____	_____

```
End Sub

Sub Switch(e, b, d)
```

```
Dim c As Integer
Dim f As Integer

e = a
f = -b
a = f
c = 1

End Sub
```

3.   Repeat the Hands-on Exercise in Section 8.2.4 on your own computer, but evaluate the function `x = Sin(x * dx) ^ dx`

9

Computations

Engineers primarily use computers to perform numerical calculations. You should already be familiar with the way in which mathematical expressions are written from your use of other programming tools, such as Excel. However, VBA differs from other languages in a few key ways. One purpose of this chapter will be to review the similarities along with pointing out the differences.

A second objective will be to review VBA's built-in functions to implement simple mathematical and trigonometric evaluations. We will also show how VBA can access the much broader range of built-in functions available in Excel. This capability greatly enhances VBA as an engineering-oriented problem-solving tool.

OBJECTIVES

After reading this chapter, you should be able to

- To construct mathematical expressions in VBA using operator priority, the left-to-right rule and parentheses.
- Understand the implications of different negation and exponentiation priorities in Excel and VBA.
- Utilize the VBA built-in functions and recognize their limitations.
- Understand the differences between Excel and VBA built-in functions.
- Know how to access Excel functions from VBA.

9.1 COMPUTATIONS

In VBA, mathematical expressions are based on three key concepts: operator priority, the left-to-right rule, and parentheses.

9.1.1 Operator Priority

VBA uses the following priorities:

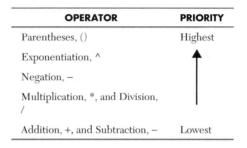

OPERATOR	PRIORITY
Parentheses, ()	Highest
Exponentiation, ^	
Negation, −	
Multiplication, *, and Division, /	
Addition, +, and Subtraction, −	Lowest

Therefore, in the expression

```
x = 5 + 7 * 2
```

the computer would first multiply 7 * 2, yielding 14 (because multiplication has a higher priority than addition), and then add that to 5, giving 19. The result would then be assigned to the variable x.

Another example is

```
z = -2 ^ 2
```

Here, the computer will first square 2, giving 4 (since exponentiation has higher a priority than negation), and then negate the 4, yielding the final answer, −4.

Remember, however, that Excel works differently. In Excel, negation has a higher priority than exponentiation. Hence, the evaluation of −2 ^ 2 in Excel would first involve negating the 2. Then the −2 would be squared, yielding 4.

Now, where is such knowledge of practical significance? The following function is used in statistics to define a bell-shaped curve:

$$y = e^{-x^2}$$

Figure 9.1 shows the curve, together with selected numerical values.

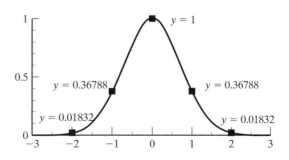

Figure 9.1. A bell-shaped curve.

The function works just fine, given the VBA rule that exponentiation has higher priority than negation. Let's examine the case where $x = -2$. In VBA, this would be written as

```
y = Exp(-2 ^ 2)
```

The exponentiation would be implemented first, giving

```
y = Exp(-4)
```

Then VBA would evaluate the exponential function at –4, yielding 0.01832, the expected result.

In contrast, if the same equation were written in Excel, the negation would be executed first. Then the negative 2 would be squared, resulting in

```
= Exp(4)
```

which would give an incorrect result of 54.598.

How could this be rectified in Excel? One way would be to use parentheses to force the exponentiation to occur first:

```
= Exp(-(2 ^ 2))
```

Alternatively, the squaring could be expressed as a multiplication:

```
= Exp(-2 * 2)
```

Then the sign wouldn't be lost, as would be the case if –2 were raised to an even integer power.

9.1.2   Left to Right

In choosing between two operations with equal priority, the computer implements them from left to right. For example, in the assignment statement

```
d = 10 / 5 * 7
```

First the computer will divide 10 by 5, yielding 2. Then it will multiply 2 * 7, giving the final answer, 14. Notice how going from right to left would give an entirely different answer:

The preceding rules can be overridden by using parentheses. That is, the computer will evaluate operations in parentheses first. For example, suppose that we want to evaluate

$$y = \frac{4+9}{7}$$

If we write it as

```
y = 4 + 9 / 7
```

the computer will first divide 9 by 7 and then add the result to 4. To force the addition to be performed first, we enclose it in parentheses thus:

```
y = (4 + 9) / 7
```

In the case of nested parentheses, the innermost ones are evaluated first:

$$r = 6 * (-3 + \underbrace{(5\hat{\ }2 - 4 * 2 * 3)}))$$
$$r = 6 * (-3 + \qquad 1 \qquad)$$
$$r = \underbrace{6 * \qquad\quad -2}$$
$$r = \qquad -12$$

9.2   BUILT-IN NUMERIC FUNCTIONS

Like Excel, VBA has built-in or intrinsic, functions for commonly employed mathematical operations. The most common numerical functions are listed in Table 9-1. Note that the spelling and implementation of some of the VBA functions differ from those in Excel. These are displayed in bold type.

TABLE 9-1   Abbreviated list of commonly used VBA built-in numeric functions, along with comparable Excel functions. The functions that differ are highlighted in boldface.

PURPOSE	VBA FUNCTION	EXCEL FUNCTION
absolute value	Abs(x)	ABS(x)
truncate to integer	Int(x)	INT(x)
round x to n digits after decimal	Round(x,n)	ROUND(x,n)
square root	**Sqr**(x)	**SQRT**(x)
exponential, e	Exp(x)	EXP(x)
natural log	**Log**(x)	**LN**(x)
base-10 log	–	LOG10(x)
base-b log	–	LOG(x,b)
value of π	–	PI()
sine	Sin(x)	SIN(x)
cosine	Cos(x)	COS(x)
tangent	Tan(x)	TAN(x)
arcsine	–	ASIN(x)
arccosine	–	ACOS(x)
arctangent	**Atn**(x)	**ATAN**(**x**)
arctangent (4 quadrant)	–	ATAN2(x,y)
degrees to radians	–	RADIANS(x)
radians to degrees	-	DEGREES(x)
x modulo y	**x Mod y**	**MOD**(**x,y**)
random number	**Rnd()**	**RAND()**

One simple examples of the use of built-in functions is to evaluate the square root of a number:

```
x = Sqr(2)
```

Another is to take the absolute value of the discriminant of the quadratic formula:

```
d = Abs(b ^ 2 - 4 * a * c)
```

You can always access VBA Help (F1) to get a full listing of the built-in functions. Simply go to the *Contents tab* and select **Visual Basic Language Reference, Functions**. You can then browse alphabetically to find a description of a particular function.

An alternative approach uses VBE's *autolist* capability. When you are typing in your code and you cannot remember a function name, merely type "VBA.". An autolist pull-down menu will appear listing all available functions in alphabetical order. If you know the first few letters of the function's name, type them, and the list will scroll down in search of a match. Once the correct function is highlighted, hit the Enter key, and the name will be typed in place of VBA.

This is a particularly handy trick, because you can invoke it without leaving the editor to search through Help.

9.2.1 Accessing Excel Functions from VBA

As is clear from Table 9.1, Microsoft Excel has many more built-in worksheet functions than VBA has. Here are a few suggestions on how you can overcome these omissions:

- The number π is unavailable in VBA. A nice trick to have VBA compute the value on the basis of the fact that $\tan(\pi/4) = 1$. Then you can determine a value of π by using the formula

  ```
  pi = 4 * Atn(1)
  ```

- Recall that trigonometric functions involving angles use or produce radian units. Degrees and radians can be converted by using the definition π radians = 180°. For example, the sine of 30° can be calculated as

  ```
  Sin(30 * pi / 180)
  ```

- Only natural logarithms are available in VBA. They can be converted to any other base by recalling that

$$\log_b(x) = \frac{\log_a(x)}{\log_a(b)}$$

  For example, the common, or base-10, logarithm of 10,000 could be calculated in VBA with

  ```
  log(10000) / log(10)
  ```

Beyond these mathematical manipulations, the *WorksheetFunction object* provides direct access to most Excel functions from within VBA (Table 9.2). For example, the following code uses the *Average* worksheet function to determine the average value of a range of cells:

```
Option Explicit
Sub AccessExcel()
Dim Answer As Double
Sheets("Sheet1").Select
Answer = Application.WorksheetFunction.Average(Range("A4:A24"))
MsgBox Answer
End Sub
```

TABLE 9-2   Partial listing of Excel worksheet functions available in VBA.[a]

MATHEMATICAL		STATISTICAL		
Acos	MInverse	Average	HarMean	Poisson
Acosh	MMult	BetaDist	HypGeomDist	Skew
Asin	Pi	BinomDist	LogNormDist	StDev
Asinh	Radians	ChiDist	Max	SumSq
Atan2	Round	ChiTest	Median	TDist
Atanh	RoundDown	Covar	Min	Trend
Cosh	RoundUp	ExponDist	Mode	Trim
Count	Sinh	FDist	NegBinomDist	TrimMean
Degrees	Slope	Fisher	NormDist	TTest
Intercept	Sum	FTest	NormInv	Var
Log	Tanh	GammaDist	Pearson	Weibull
Log10	Transpose	GeoMean	Percentile	ZTest

a. To see a list of all the available worksheet functions, go to the *Help Answer Wizard* and enter *List of Worksheet Functions Available to Visual Basic*. To see a complete description of how to access Excel functions, enter *Using Microsoft Excel Worksheet Functions in Visual Basic*.

You can also insert a worksheet function directly into a cell by specifying the function as the value of the *Formula property* of the corresponding *Range* object. In the following codes, the *Average* worksheet function is assigned to the *Formula* property of range A1 on Sheet1 in the active workbook:

```
Sheets("Sheet1").Select
Range("A1").Formula = "=Average(A4:A24)"
```

Finally, you can use the built-in Excel functions directly in VBA formulas. For example, the volume of a liquid in a hollow horizontal cylinder of radius *r*, length *L*, and depth *h* is computed mathematically as

$$V = \left[r^2 \cos^{-1}\left(\frac{r-h}{r} \right) - (r-h)\sqrt{2rh - h^2} \right] L$$

Because there is no inverse cosine function in VBA, you would be forced to compute it with the inverse tangent.[1] However, Excel's inverse cosine can be accessed directly, as in the code

```
V =(r ^ 2 * Application.WorksheetFunction.Acos((r - h) / r) _

                 - (r - h) * Sqr(2 * r * h - h ^ 2)) * L
```

KEY TERMS

Autolist	Formula property	Stokes' law
Average worksheet function	Range object	von Karman equation
Contents tab	Redlich-Kwong equation	Worksheet function object
Fanning friction factor	Reynolds number (R_e)	

Problems

1. What value would y have after the following formula was implemented In VBA?

   ```
   y = Sin(100 * Atn(1) / 150)
   ```

   Explain your result.

2. Without using ^0.5 to implement the square-root function ($\sqrt{\ }$), write a VBA expression for each of the following mathematical formulas:

   (a) $\quad y = \sqrt{\dfrac{5\cos x}{2y}}$

   (b) $\quad b = -\dfrac{\sqrt{5x}}{\sin x - 2a}$

   (c) $\quad y = \dfrac{3x}{4\sin y}$

   (d) $\quad y = \dfrac{\sin x}{2a}$

   (e) $\quad y = \dfrac{\pi}{h}\sqrt{h^2 + \dfrac{r^2}{a}}$

3. In VBA and Excel, multiple exponentiation is implemented in a left-to-right fashion. For example,

   $$2^{3^4}$$

   would be implemented as

   $$2 \wedge 3 \wedge 4 \rightarrow 8 \wedge 4 \rightarrow 1024$$

   In contrast, Fortran 90 (a popular computer language used extensively by engineers) uses a right-to-left approach.[2] Thus,

   $$2**3**4 \rightarrow 2**81 \rightarrow 2.41785 \times 10^2$$

---

[1] The formula is

$$\cos^{-1} x = \frac{\pi}{2} - \tan^{-1}\left(\frac{x}{\sqrt{1-x^2}}\right).$$

[2] Fortran 90 uses double asterisks to designate exponentiation.

Which approach is most natural from a mathematical perspective? Defend your choice.

4. The *Redlich–Kwong equation* predicts the true behavior of a gas better than the ideal-gas law by inserting terms which describe molecular interactions that occur at high pressures. The equation is

$$p = \frac{RT}{(v-b)} - \frac{a}{v(v+b)\sqrt{T}}$$

where

$$a = 0.427 \frac{R^2 T_c^{2.5}}{p_c} \quad \text{and} \quad b = 0.0866 R \frac{T_c}{p_c}$$

Write VBA expressions for these formulas. Make certain that they are in the correct sequence to compute the pressure correctly.

5. The *Fanning friction factor f* for turbulent fluid flow in a pipe can be determined by solving for the root of the *von Karman equation*

$$F(f) = 4 \log_{10}\left(R_e \sqrt{f}\right) - 0.4 - \frac{1}{\sqrt{f}}$$

where R_e is called the *Reynolds number*. How would the right-hand side of this equation be written in VBA?

6. Suppose that you place a spherical particle in a beaker containing a quiescent fluid (Figure 9.2). The settling velocity of the particle can be estimated with *Stokes' law*,

$$v = \frac{g}{18}\left(\frac{\rho_p - \rho_f}{\mu}\right)d^2$$

where v is the downward velocity of the particle [cm/s], g is the acceleration due to gravity [$\cong 980$ cm/s], ρ_p is the density of the particle [g/cm^3], ρ_f is the density of the fluid [g/cm^3], μ is the dynamic viscosity of the fluid [g/(cm s)], and d is the particle's diameter [cm].

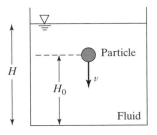

Figure 9.2.

If the particle is initially placed at a depth of H_0 in the fluid, develop a well-structured Sub procedure named *Stokes* to calculate how long it will take the particle to reach the bottom or top of the beaker. Your program should have the following characteristics:

- Place an Option Explicit statement prior to your Sub procedure, and use Dim statements to assign appropriate data types to all variables.
- Enter all the parameters on a worksheet entitled *Input Data*.
- Include a Function procedure to calculate the velocity of the particle.
- Use a Const statement to assign the value and set the data type of g. Make g available throughout the whole module.
- Display the settling velocity in a worksheet cell on the *Input Data* sheet.
- If the settling velocity is positive, use a message box to display the time it takes the particle to reach the bottom of the beaker. Otherwise, display the time it takes to reach the top.

Employ the following parameters for the beaker and the particle: $H = 20$ cm, $H_0 = 10$ cm, $g = 980$ cm/s^2, and $d = 0.05$ cm. Use the following fluid–particle combinations to test your program:

Fluid	ρ_f (g/cm³)	μ (g/(cm s)	Particle	ρ_p (g/cm³)
Water @ 4 °C	1	0.0157	Ice	0.92
Mercury @ 20 °C	13.55	0.0015	Platinum	21.45
SAE 10W 30 @ 38 °C	0.88	0.067	Rock	2.65
Seawater @ 10 °C	1.026	0.00131	Cork	0.12

10

Strings and Dialog Boxes

In a similar way that numbers are manipulated, strings can also be manipulated by operators and built-in functions. For example, VBA includes functions that allow you to either paste or parse strings. These manipulations have a variety of applications including the effective display of information to users. The first part of this chapter describes some of these functions.

The second part shows how to capitalize on these capabilities in the context of message and input boxes. This material also describes several enhanced features of message and input boxes. These include placing multiple buttons on message boxes.

OBJECTIVES

After reading this chapter, you should be able to

- Use VBA string functions to concatenate and parse strings.
- Change the case of a string.
- Create the buttons and messages in Message Boxes.
- Understand how data typing relates to Input Box buttons.

10.1 STRING FUNCTIONS AND MANIPULATIONS

VBA has an extensive array of functions that manipulate strings. The most commonly used ones are summarized in Table 10-1.

TABLE 10-1 Abbreviated list of commonly used VBA built-in string functions.

Function	Description
InStr(*string1*, *string2*)	Returns the position of *string1* within *string2*
LCase(*string*)	Converts *string* to lowercase.
Left(*string*, *length*)	Returns a specified number of characters (*length*) from the left side of *string*.
Len(*string*)	Returns the number of characters in *string*.
LTrim(*string*)	Returns *string* without leading spaces.
Mid(*string*, *start*[, *length*])	Returns *length** characters from *string*, beginning at *start*.
Right(*string*, *length*)	Returns *length* characters from the right side of *string*.
RTrim(*string*)	Returns *string* without trailing spaces.
Space(*number*)	Returns a string consisting of *number* spaces.
Str(*number*)	Returns the string representation of *number*.
Trim(*string*)	Returns *string* without leading and trailing spaces.
UCase(*string*)	Converts *string* to uppercase.
Val(*string*)	Returns the number contained in *string* as a numeric value.

* If *length* is omitted or if there are fewer than *length* characters in the text (including the character at *start*), all characters, from the starting position to the end of the string, are returned.

10.1.1 Concatenating and Parsing Strings

String functions have many applications, but they are especially useful for making interfaces more user friendly. Such applications often involve pasting strings together. This process, which is formally called *concatenation*, uses the operator &. For example, suppose we assign strings to a pair of variables, as in the code

```
a = "Go"
b = "away!"
```

We can paste the strings together with the assignment statement

```
c = a & b
```

The value "Goaway!" would then be stored in c. A space can be added between the two words by pasting a blank space between them:

```
c = a & " " & b
```

If we used a message box to display the value of c, we would write

```
MsgBox c
```

and the result would be

Another example relates to dividing up a string in order to display a personalized message. First, let's suppose that a name is assigned to a variable:

```
nam = "Doe, Jane"
```

We can determine the number of characters in this string (including blanks) by using the *Len function*:

```
y = Len(nam)
```

In this case, y would be equal to 9. Then, we could use the *InStr* function to determine the position of the comma:

```
x = InStr(nam, ",")
```

The first argument specifies the string expression being searched (nam) and the second the string expression sought. Since the comma appears in the fourth position, x would be assigned a value of 4. The *Left function* could then be used to lop the individual's last name off of nam:

```
surname = Left(nam, x - 1)
```

The *Right function* could be used in a similar fashion to obtain the first name:

```
prename = Right(nam, y - x - 1)
```

The first and last names can then be concatenated with a few phrases to display a personalized message:

```
MsgBox "Dear " & prename & " " & surname & ", Howdy!"
```

The result would look like this:

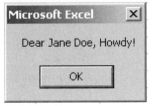

10.1.2 LCase and UCase

The *LCase* and *UCase* functions return a string expression with all letters in lowercase and uppercase, respectively. The following procedure illustrates how these statements work:

```
Option Explicit
Sub CaseManip()
```

```
Dim a As String, au As String, al As String
a = "Joe Pass"
au = UCase(a)
al = LCase(a)
MsgBox a & " " & au & " " & al
End Sub
```

When the Sub is run, the following messages are displayed:

A nice application of these functions involves user queries. Suppose that you set up an input box to ask whether the user wants to employ metric or English units in a computation:

```
Option Explicit
Sub QueryManip()
Dim ans As String
ans = InputBox("metric or English?", "Units?")
If ans = "metric" Then
  unit = "meter"
Else
  unit = "foot"
End If
msgbox unit
End Sub
```

Now, what if the user happens to enter "Metric"?

Because "Metric" is not the same as "metric", the result will be incorrect:

Using the LCase function in the InputBox statement provides a nice remedy:

```
ans = LCase(InputBox("metric or English?", "Units?"))
```

Regardless of the capitalization, the value entered by the user would be converted to lowercase, and the If statement would yield the desired result. For example, the user could enter "mEtRiC", and the code would still work properly, displaying

10.2   MESSAGE BOXES

We have used message boxes extensively throughout this book. Now let's look at their syntax and capabilities in more detail. A simplified representation of the syntax of a message box is

```
MsgBox prompt[, buttons] [, title]
```

where *prompt* is a String expression displayed as the message in the dialog box (prompt can be up to approximately 1024 characters, depending on their width, *buttons* is an optional argument that sets up the buttons on the message box (if you omit it, the default is the OK button), and *title* is an optional string expression displayed in the title bar of the dialog box (if you omit it, the default is the application name).

The simplest application is to display a message with no frills:

```
MsgBox "Click OK to Continue"
```

When this statement is implemented, the following message box will appear on the screen:

When the user clicks OK, the program proceeds to the statement following the MsgBox statement. Note that, because we didn't specify a title type, the application name, Microsoft Excel, is displayed as the default title.

If you display a very long message, VBA will automatically wrap the text around after about 128 characters. For example, the code

```
Option Explicit
Sub LongMsg()
Dim msg As String, msg1 As String, msg2 As String
Dim msg3 As String, msg4 As String, msg5 As String
Dim msg6 As String
msg1 = "The following program is designed to compute "
```

```
msg2 = "the velocity of a falling parachutist "
msg3 = "based on Newton's Second Law. "
msg4 = "The model is v = cd * g / m * (1 - Exp(-cd / m * t)) "
msg5 = "All units are in the MKS system. "
msg6 = "Please proceed by clicking OK."
msg = msg1 & msg2 & msg3 & msg4 & msg5 & msg6
MsgBox msg
End Sub
```

will result in the following display:

You can control the display by inserting a carriage return character, Chr(13), wherever you want to break a line. For example, your message could be rewritten as

```
msg = msg1 & msg2 & msg3 & Chr(13) & msg4 & Chr(13) & _
msg5 & Chr(13) & msg6
```

with the result

Messages can also be enhanced by adding supplementary information to the message and by adding a title:

```
velocity = 24.5
Msg = "The Velocity is " & velocity & " m/s"
Title = "Parachutist Problem"
MsgBox Msg, , Title
```

When this code is implemented, the following message box will appear on the screen:

This message box provides the user with a numerical result, plus additional information (such as units). Because we did not specify a *button*, that argument is omitted (as signified by the empty space between the two commas).

10.2.1 Buttons

VBA provides you with several possibilities for buttons (Table 10-2). The first group of values (0–5) describes the number and type of buttons displayed in the dialog box, the second group (16, 32, 48, 64) describes the icon style, and the third group (0, 256, 512) determines which button is the default—that is, which will be highlighted so that it will be automatically chosen if you hit the Enter key. When adding numbers to create a final value for the *button* argument, use only one number from each group. Note that the constant values (like vbOKOnly) can be used in place of the numerical values.

TABLE 10-2 Built-in constants for use with the button argument of the MsgBox function.

		Constant Value	
Category	Description	String	Numeric
Number and type	Display OK button only.	vbOKOnly	0
	Display OK and Cancel buttons.	vbOKCancel	1
	Display Abort, Retry, and Ignore buttons.	vbAbortRetryIgnore	2
	Display Yes, No, and Cancel buttons.	vbYesNoCancel	3
	Display Yes and No buttons.	vbYesNo	4
	Display Retry and Cancel buttons.	vbRetryCancel	5
Icon style	Display Critical Message icon.	vbCritical	16
	Display Warning Query icon.	vbQuestion	32
	Display Warning Message icon.	vbExclamation	48
	Display Information Message icon.	vbInformation	64
Default buttons	First button is default.	vbDefaultButton1	0
	Second button is default.	vbDefaultButton2	256
	Third button is default.	vbDefaultButton3	512
	Fourth button is default	vbDefaultButton4	768

As an example, suppose that we wanted a message box with *Yes, No,* and *Cancel* buttons and the *Warning Query* icon. We could then write

```
MsgBox "Do it again?", vbYesNoCancel + vbQuestion
```

The resulting message box would look like this:

By using the corresponding numeric constants from Table 10-2, the following code results in the same message box being displayed:

```
MsgBox "Do it again?", 3 + 32
```

Adding the numeric constants, of course, yields the same message box, too:

```
MsgBox "Do it again?", 35
```

You should recognize that when the default OK button is used, clicking it merely means that the next line in the macro will be executed. In contrast, when two or more buttons are included, a unique value will be returned, based on the one you clicked. This information would then form the basis for triggering some action. In these cases, the syntax is changed slightly to

```
v = MsgBox(prompt[, buttons] [, title])
```

where v is a variable to which a constant value representing the choice of button is assigned. The constants are summarized in Table 10-3. In this case, the message box acts like a function (i.e., it returns a value). Hence, the parentheses must be included.

TABLE 10-3 Constants returned from button selection.

String	Numeric	Description
vbOK	1	OK
vbCancel	2	Cancel
vbAbort	3	Abort
vbRetry	4	Retry
vbIgnore	5	Ignore
vbYes	6	Yes
vbNo	7	No

As an example, the code

```
Msg = "Do you want to continue ?"
Style = vbYesNo + vbQuestion + vbDefaultButton2
Title = "MsgBox Demo"      ' Define title.
Response = MsgBox(Msg, Style, Title)
```

results in the following message box:

When the user clicks on one of the buttons, a value will be returned and assigned to the variable `Response`. For example, if the user clicked on "Yes", the variable `Response` would be set equal to `VbYes`, or 6. Therefore, you could make a decision, such as the following, on the basis of the result:

```
Response = MsgBox(Msg, Style, Title)
If Response = vbYes Then
```

```
    MyString = "Yes"
Else
    MyString = "No"
End If
```

Alternatively, the same action could be programmed as follows:

```
Response = MsgBox(Msg, Style, Title)
If Response = 6 Then
    MyString = "Yes"
Else
    MyString = "No"
End If
```

10.3 INPUT BOXES

The *input box* is handy for obtaining a single value from the user. A simplified representation of its syntax is

```
v = InputBox(prompt[, title] [, default])
```

where *v* is a variable to which the input value entered by the user is assigned, *prompt* is a string expression displayed as the message in the dialog box (*prompt* can be up to approximately 1024 characters), *title* is an optional string expression displayed in the title bar of the dialog box (if you omit it, the default is the application name), and *default* is a string expression displayed in the text box as the default response. If you omit if, the text box is displayed empty.

The simplest application is to display a message with no frills:

```
UsersName = InputBox("Please enter your name")
```

When this statement is implemented, the following box will appear on the screen:

When the user enters a name and clicks OK, the value will be returned to your program and assigned to the variable `UsersName`.

A more complex example is

```
Msg = "Please enter the initial velocity"
Velocity = InputBox(Msg, "Velocity (m/s)", 0)
```

resulting in the message box

In this case, along with the message, we now include a title (showing the proper units) and a suggested initial velocity of zero.

10.3.1 Hands-on Exercise: Data Typing, String Functions, and Input Boxes

When one uses input boxes, subtle problems can arise that relate to the issue of data typing. Let's now explore such problems and how they can be rectified.

STEP 1: Open a new workbook, go to the VBE, and insert a module. Set up an input box to enter a value for velocity into a program by entering the following into the code window:

```
Option Explicit
Sub test()
Dim v As Double
v = InputBox("Units: m/s", "Enter velocity:")
End Sub
```

When this program is run, the following message box is displayed:

Enter the number 10 and hit **OK** to check that the macro is running properly.

STEP 2: Suppose now that you run the program again and hit cancel when the message box appears. In this case, a run-time error should occur:

Microsoft Visual Basic

Run-time error '13':

Type mismatch

| Continue | End | Debug | Help |

What happened? The error message "Type mismatch" is our first clue. This error means that we are attempting to store a constant of one type into a variable of a different type. So it appears that the constant which is brought back when Cancel is hit is of a data type different from that of the double-precision variable v to which the constant is assigned.

STEP 3: To find out what has occurred, remove the Option Explicit and the Dim statements from the code:

```
Sub test()
v = InputBox("Units: m/s", "Enter velocity:")
End Sub
```

Now use the F8 key to step through the program until the Input Box is displayed. Strike the cancel key. In this case, an error does not occur. Place the cursor over the variable v, with the following result:

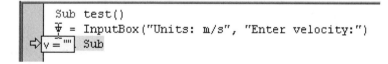

```
Sub test()
v = InputBox("Units: m/s", "Enter velocity:")
    v = ""   Sub
```

So when the Cancel button is hit, a *zero-length string* ("") is returned. Consequently, the Input Box statement involves assigning a string constant (a "square peg") to a numeric variable (a "round hole"). Hence, a "type mismatch" error is induced.

STEP 4: A number of remedies can be devised. One straightforward solution to the problem uses the Val function. Recall from Table 10-1 that this function returns the numbers contained in a string as a numeric value of the appropriate type. Accordingly, add the Val function, and put back the Option Explicit and the Dim statement. The revised code would look like this:

```
Option Explicit
Sub test()
Dim v As Double
v = Val(InputBox("Units: m/s", "Enter velocity:"))
End Sub
```

When you step through this program and hit Cancel, no error occurs:

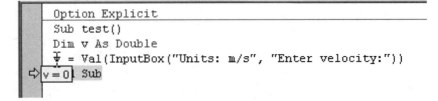

The reason no error occurs is that the Val function converts the null string "" to its numerical equivalent, zero.

This "fix" certainly solves the immediate problem of allowing us to use the Cancel button. But suppose that assigning a zero to v would cause subsequent problems. Such would be the case if zero could actually be a realistic input value for the velocity. Consequently, you wouldn't know whether the user actually intended to enter zero or, rather, wanted to strike the Cancel button.

STEP 5: One way to handle this case is represented by the following code:

```
Option Explicit
Sub test()
Dim vtemp As Variant, v As Double
vtemp = InputBox("Units: m/s", "Enter velocity:")
If vtemp = "" Then
   End
Else
   v = Val(vtemp)
End If
End Sub
```

Note how the temporary variable vtemp is dimensioned as Variant so that it can hold either string or numeric constants. Then, if a null string is returned, the program terminates. Otherwise, v is converted to double precision by the Val function.

KEY TERMS

Button	Left function
Concatenation	Len function
Input box	Right function
InStr function	UCase function
LCase function	Zero-length string ("")

Problems

1. Given that mass (stored in the variable m) has a value of 20 kg, write the VBA code that will make the following appear on the screen:

2. Fill in the blanks in the VBA Sub procedure so that the following message box is
    displayed (notice that the "No" button is highlighted):

```
Option Explicit
Sub test()
Dim ans As String
ans = _____
End Sub
```

3. Fill in the blanks in the VBA Sub procedure

```
Option Explicit
Sub Test()
Dim pop As Long
pop = _____
End Sub
```

so that the following input box is displayed:

4. Develop a procedure that uses an InputBox to obtain a name from a user. Then
    have the procedure manipulate the name so that its first letter is capitalized and
    all following letters are lowercase. Display the result with a MsgBox. Test the pro-
    cedure by entering a name in capital letters.

5. Develop a short VBA Sub procedure to compute the settling velocity of a spherical particle by means of Stokes' law,

$$v = \frac{g}{18}\left(\frac{\rho_p - \rho_f}{\mu}\right)d^2$$

where v is the downward velocity of the particle [cm/s], g is the acceleration due to gravity [$\cong$980 cm/s], ρ_p is the density of the particle [g/cm^3], ρ_f is the density of the fluid [g/cm^3], μ is the dynamic viscosity of the fluid [g/(cm s)], and d is the particle's diameter [cm]. Design the program for small mineral particles ($\rho_p = 2.65$ g/cm^3) settling in freshwater ($\mu = 0.013$ g/(cm s) and $\rho_f = 1$ g/cm^3). Use an input box to enter the particle's diameter and a message box to display the particle's velocity to three decimal places in units of m/d. Make the boxes user friendly by including units and titles.

6. Store the months of the year in a string variable, `month`, as in

    `month = "janfebmaraprmayjunjulaugsepoctnovdec"`

    Have the user enter a date in the following format:

    `08/05/1948`

    Design a program that uses `month` to display the date as

    `Aug. 5, 1948`

11

Structured Programming: Decisions

The simplest of all computer programs perform instructions sequentially. That is, the program statements are executed line by line, starting at the top of the program and moving down to the end. Because a strict sequence is highly limiting, all computer languages include statements allowing programs to take nonsequential paths, classified as follows:

- *Decisions* (or *Selection*). The branching of flow based on a decision.
- *Loops* (or *Repetition*). The looping of flow to allow statements to be repeated.

This chapter deals with branching instructions, or statements that reroute the flow of logic to a line or statement other than the next in sequence.

SECTIONS

- 11.1 Structured Programming
- 11.2 Flowcharts
- 11.3 The If/Then/Else Decision Structure
- 11.4 If/Then/Elseif Structure
- 11.5 Select Case Structure
- 11.6 Nesting
- 11.7 Compound Logical Expressions

OBJECTIVES

After reading this chapter, you should be able to

- Understand why structured programming results in clear and coherent code.
- Translate from a flowchart to a VBA representation of an algorithm.
- Understand where single line If statements are appropriate.
- Create decisions with If/Then/Else and Select Case constructs.
- Recognize when an If/Then/Elseif construct is required.
- Understand the difference between an If/Then/Elseif and a Select Case construct.
- Nest control structures within each other.
- Appreciate how indentation enhances the clarity of your programs.
- Evaluate complex compound logical expressions using priority rules.
- Understand how logical complements and De Morgan's Theorem can be used to simplify and clarify the meaning of logical expressions.

11.1 STRUCTURED PROGRAMMING

Although selection can greatly enhance the power and flexibility of your programs, its indiscriminate and undisciplined application can introduce enormous complexity into a program. In the early days of computer programming, the major culprit was the *GoTo statement*, which allows you to directly override the sequence in which the program is executed. The general form of this statement is

```
GoTo line-identifier
```

where *line-identifier* denotes the line that is to be executed next. The following VBA code fragment illustrates how the instruction works:

```
    x = InputBox("enter a value")
    GoTo 1
    MsgBox x
    1: c = x + 8
```

After entering the value of x, the program would normally advance to the Msgbox statement. However, because of the GoTo, the program jumps to the statement labeled 1.

Although such jumping around might seem innocuous, the indiscriminate use of GoTo statements can lead to programs that are extremely difficult to understand, debug, and maintain. Such programs are referred to as *spaghetti codes,* because their logic resembles a plate of spaghetti.[1]

As a consequence, computer scientists have developed a number of conventions to impose order on nonsequential algorithms and make the GoTo statement obsolete. These conventions are collectively called *structured programming.* Some actually involve special VBA statements that provide clear and coherent ways to perform selection. Such statements are called *control structures.* There are three basic types of decision structures used in VBA:

1. If/Then/Else structures

2. Cascade structures (If/Then/ElseIf)

3. Case structures (Select Case)

Figure 11.1 is a dramatic example of the contrast between unstructured and structured approaches. Both programs are designed to determine the average of a group of values. Although the programs compute identical results, their designs differ starkly. The logic of the unstructured program in Figure 11.1*a* is not obvious; the user must delve into the code on a line-by-line basis to decipher the program.

In contrast, the major parts of Figure 11.2*b* are immediately apparent. Program execution progresses in an orderly fashion from the top to the bottom with no major jumps. Every segment has one entrance and one exit, and each is clearly delineated by spaces and indentation.

---

[1] In Australia, they're referred to as *kangaroo codes* for obvious reasons.

```
Sub Spaghetti( )                        Sub Structured( )
1: g = InputBox("Enter value:")         'Sum and count values
If g < 0 Then GoTo 2                     Do
s = s + g                                   g = InputBox("Enter value:")
i = i + 1                                   If g < 0 Then Exit Do
GoTo 1                                       s = s + g
2: If i = 0 Then GoTo 3                      i = i + 1
a = s / i                               Loop
GoTo 4                                   'Compute the average
3: a = 0                                 If i > 0 Then
4: MsgBox a                                 a = s / i
End Sub                                  Else
                                            a = 0
                                         End If
                                         MsgBox a
                                         End Sub
```

(*a*) Unstructured   (*b*) Structured

Figure 11.1.   Contrast between (*a*) unstructured and (*b*) structured versions of the same algorithm.

11.2   FLOWCHARTS

A visual or graphical representation of an algorithm, a *flowchart* is an ideal vehicle for visualizing some of the fundamental control structures employed in computer programming. The flowchart employs a series of blocks and arrows, each of which represents a particular operation or step in the algorithm (Figure 11.2). The arrows represent the sequence in which the operations are implemented.

SYMBOL	NAME	FUNCTION
	Terminal	Represents the beginning or end of a program.
	Flow lines	Represent the flow of logic. The humps on the horizontal arrow indicate that it passes over and does not connect with the vertical flow lines.
	Process	Represents calculations or data manipulations.
	Input/output	Represents inputs or outputs of data and information.
	Decision	Represents a comparison, question, or other condition that determines alternative paths to be followed.
	Count-controlled loop	Used for loops that repeat a prespecified number of iterations.
	Junction	Represents the confluence of flow lines.
	Off-page connector	Represents a break that is continued on another page.

Figure 11.2.   Symbols Used in Flowcharts

Figure 11.3*a* shows a flowchart for a simple algorithm that adds two numbers and displays the result. The algorithm begins at the Start box and then proceeds sequentially to two parallelogram-shaped input/output boxes to input the numbers to be added: *a* and *b*. Next, a rectangular-shaped process box is used to add the numbers and assign the result to the variable *c*. An output box indicates that the sum is displayed. Finally, the algorithm terminates at the end block. In contrast to the corresponding VBA code (Figure 11.3*b*), notice how the flowchart is unencumbered by details and concentrates on the sequence of the key steps in the algorithm.

Although this algorithm is very simple, it illustrates how the computer proceeds sequentially from statement to statement. As in the sections that follow, the flowchart's true utility is demonstrated when a program's flow is non-sequential.

11.3 THE IF/THEN/ELSE DECISION STRUCTURE

The *If/Then/Else structure* has the syntax

```
If condition Then
   [truestatements]
[Else
   [falsestatements]]
End If
```

where `condition` is a logical expression that evaluates to True or False, `truestatements` are one or more statements that are executed if the `condition` is True, and `falsestatements` are one or more statements that are executed if the `condition` is False.

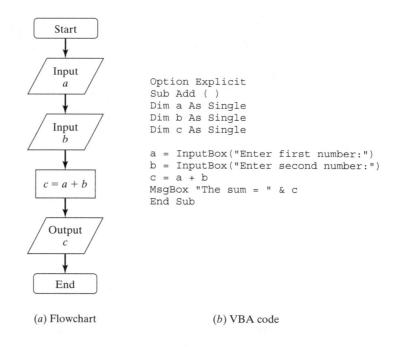

(*a*) Flowchart   (*b*) VBA code

Figure 11.3.   (*a*) A flowchart and (*b*) corresponding VBA code.

The simplest form of the `condition` is a single relational expression that compares two values, as in the general representation

$$value_1 \ relation \ value_2$$

where `values` can be constants, variables, or expressions and `relation` is one of the relational operators listed in Table 11-1.

Figure 11.4 shows a flowchart of the If/Then/Else structure, along with an example of its use. In this case, if the variable a is less than zero, we use the Abs function to allow the square root to be evaluated. If a is greater than or equal to zero, the square root of a can be evaluated directly.

TABLE 11-1 Summary of relational operators in VBA.

EXAMPLE	OPERATOR	RELATIONSHIP
`var = 0`	=	Equals or Is equal to
`unit <> "m"`	<>	Is not equal to
`var < 0`	<	Is less than
`x > y`	>	Is greater than
`3.9 <= x / 3`	<=	Is less than or equal to
`var >= 0`	>=	Is greater than or equal to

11.3.1 Indentation

Notice how the actual statements denoting the true and the false events are indented for clarity. In all my own programs, I use an indentation of two spaces. If you indent only one space, the indentation will be difficult to perceive. On the other hand, three or more spaces can represent overkill. For example, some individuals use the tab to indent. In the VBE, the default indentation setting is four spaces. For computer code with many indentations, this may result in the code extending off the screen. You can change the default indentation to two spaces by making the menu selection **Tools, Options**, selecting the *Editor tab*, and changing *Tab Width:* field to 2:

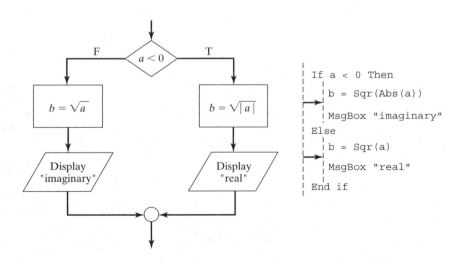

Figure 11.4.   If/Then/Else Block Structure

11.3.2 Single Decision Structure (If/Then)

In cases where there is no false alternative, the *If/Then/Else structure* can be simplified by dropping the Else clause, as in

```
If condition Then
   [truestatements]
End If
```

Figure 11.5 shows a flowchart of the structure, along with an example of its use. In this case, we are protecting against a division by zero. If the variable a is not equal to zero, we perform a division and display the result as a message box. Otherwise, the division is not implemented.

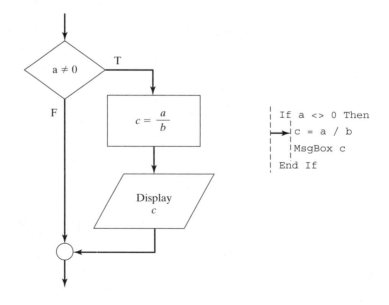

Figure 11.5. If/Then Block Structure

Suppose you develop a program that requires the user to enter a value for the mass of an object into a worksheet cell, say, B5. The VBA code to fetch this value into your program and assign it to a variable m can be written as

```
Range("b5").Select
m = ActiveCell.Value
```

Clearly, an object's mass cannot be less than or equal to zero. Consequently, it would be nice to prevent the user from entering a mass that was less than or equal to zero.

The If/Then structure provides a neat way to detect whether a user's input contains such errors. The following code is illustrative:

```
'Error trap to prevent a negative or zero mass
If m <= 0 Then
  MsgBox "mass must be greater than zero"
  Range("b5").Select
  End
End If
```

If a positive value is entered in cell b5, the program will immediately skip to the End If statement and proceed with the remainder of the program. If an incorrect value (i.e., a negative number or zero) is entered, the following message box appears:

The preceding code does three nice things:

1. It provides the user with constructive feedback in the form of an error message.
2. It places the active cell at the location that needs to be fixed (b5).
3. It terminates execution of the sub so that the user can correct the mistake and run the program again.

11.3.3 Single-Line If Statement

The If/Then/Else structure can be simplified even further when single statements are triggered by the logical condition. The syntax for such a *single-line If statement* is

```
If condition Then [truestatement] [Else falsestatement]
```

The statement operates as follows: If `condition` is True, the statement following Then is executed. If `condition` is False, the statement following Else is executed.

As an example, suppose that if a variable is greater than 0, we would like to set it to 1. Otherwise, we would like to set it to –1. The following single-line If statement accomplishes this manipulation:

```
If x > 0 Then x = 1 Else x = -1
```

In this example, something happens in the case of both the True (x > 0) and the False (x ≤ 0) option. Note that the statement fits on a single line; that is not always so.

Observe that single-line Ifs must have a `truestatement`, whereas the `Else` `falsestatement` is optional. If it is left out and the condition is false, nothing happens and the program moves to the next statement. A simple example would be to take the absolute value of a negative number:

```
If x < 0 Then x = Abs(x)
```

In this case, if x is negative, it will be made positive. If x is greater than or equal to zero, nothing happens.

Although single-line Ifs are useful for short, simple tests, when either the true or the false option consists of more than one statement, the multiline If/Then/Else structure is required.

11.4   IF/THEN/ELSEIF STRUCTURE

It often happens that the false option of an If/Then/Else is another decision, as, for example, when we have more than two options for a particular problem. In such cases, a special form of decision structure, the *If/Then/ElseIf*, is used. This structure has the general syntax

```
If condition1 Then
  [truestatements1]
[ElseIf condition2 Then
  [truestatements2]
[ElseIf condition3 Then
  [truestatements3]
[Else
  [falsestatements]]
End If
```

As an example, suppose that you want to determine the sign of a number. There are three possible outcomes: positive, negative, and zero. One way to find the sign would be to test the number and, if it is positive, assign a value of 1 to another variable. Otherwise, the number either has a negative sign (assign –1) or is zero (assign 0). A second If/Then/Else structure can be used to test the three possibilities:

```
If x > 0 Then
  'positive
  s = 1
Else
  'negative or zero
  If x < 0 Then
    'negative
    s = -1
  Else
    'zero
    s = 0
  End If
End If
```

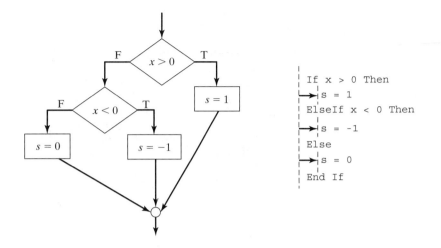

Figure 11.6. If/Then/ElseIf Structure

Although this structure is perfectly acceptable, notice that the False option (Else) leads to an If statement. Consequently, the test could also be programmed as an If/Then/ElseIf:

```
If x > 0 Then
  'positive
  s = 1
ElseIf x < 0 Then
  'negative
  s = -1
Else
  'zero
  s = 0
End If
```

Now, since both versions work identically, why is the second superior to the first? Aside from the fact that it uses fewer lines, there is a more important reason: The second structure *communicates better*. The first structure makes it look like numbers can be thought of as being in two major categories: positive and zero/negative. A more natural way to look at numbers is let them fall into three categories: positive, negative, and zero. The If/Then/ElseIf captures this idea of equal categories better than the If/Then/Else does.

The If/Then/ElseIf structure is sometimes called a *cascade structure* because of the way that the false options resemble a cascade of decisions. The notion of a cascade is reinforced by the flowchart representation of the If/Then/ElseIf, as in Figure 11.6.

11.5 SELECT CASE STRUCTURE

The *Select Case structure* just takes the If/Then/ElseIf to its logical conclusion. That is, it is best in situations where we execute particular actions on the basis of the value of a single variable. The general format of the Select Case structure is

```
Select Case testexpression
  [Case expressionlist1
    [statements]]
```

```
   [Case expressionlist2
     [statements]]
   [Case Else
     [elsestatements]]
End Select
```

A nice example is the translation of a numerical grade into a letter grade in a course. Using the Select Case construct, one might write the following code:

```
Select Case grade
  Case Is >= 90
    g = "A"
  Case Is >= 80
    g = "B"
  Case Is >= 70
    g = "C"
  Case Is >= 60
    g = "D"
  Case Else
    g = "F"
End Select
```

The flowchart for the Select Case structure is illustrated in Figure 11.7.

You can use multiple expressions or ranges in each Case clause. For example, the following line is valid:

```
Case 1 To 4, 7 To 9, 11, 13, Is > MaxNumber
```

You also can specify ranges and multiple expressions for character strings. In the following example, Case matches strings that are exactly equal to everything, strings that fall between nuts and soup in alphabetic order, and the current value of a Boolean variable, TestItem:

```
Case "everything", "nuts" To "soup", TestItem
```

11.5.1 If/Then/ElseIf Versus Select Case

In many instances, the If/Then/ElseIf and Select Case structures can be employed for the same purpose. For example, the previous code translating numerical grades into letter grades can also be programmed as

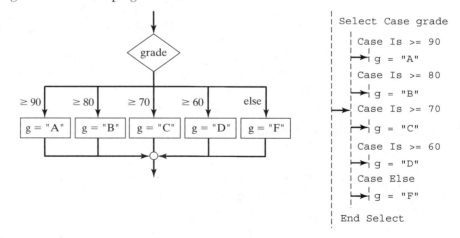

Figure 11.7. Select Case Structure

```
If grade >= 90 Then
  g = "A"
ElseIf grade >= 80 Then
  g = "B"
ElseIf grade >= 70 Then
  g = "C"
ElseIf grade >= 60 Then
  g = "D"
Else
  g = "F"
End If
```

In such situations, I usually prefer the Select Case structure, because, when I see it, I know that I'm dealing with a decision that hinges on the value of a single variable.

Although the Select Case and If/Then/ElseIf are often interchangeable, there are instances in which the If/Then/ElseIf is superior. In particular, it is preferable when the decision depends on more than one variable. Suppose that you're designing a control mechanism for a heating and cooling system for a building that is governed by the following rules:

- If the temperature is greater than 85°F, turn on the air-conditioning.
- If the temperature and the humidity are both greater than 80°F, turn on the air-conditioning.
- If the temperature is less than 65°F, turn on the heat.

The If/Then/ElseIf can be used to program this set of conditions neatly as

```
If temperature > 85 Then
  MsgBox "Cool"
ElseIf temperature > 80 and humidity > 80 Then
  MsgBox "Cool"
ElseIf temperature < 65 Then
  MsgBox "Heat"
End If
```

Although the Select Case structure could be used, it is more verbose and must, in fact, include If/Then statements:

```
Select Case temperature
  Case Is >= 85
    MsgBox "Cool"
  Case Is >= 80
    If Humidity > 80 Then
      MsgBox "Cool"
    End If
  Case Is < 65
    MsgBox "Heat"
End Select
```

11.6 NESTING

Structures can be *nested* within each other. A good example is the code used to determine the roots of the quadratic equation

$$f(x) = ax^2 + bx + c \qquad (11\text{-}1)$$

Top-down design provides a nice approach to designing an appropriate algorithm. *Top-down design* involves programming the general structure of the algorithm and then refining the algorithm by inserting details. To start, we must recognize that, depending on whether the parameter *a* in the quadratic formula is zero, we will either have "weird" cases (e.g., single roots or trivial values) or conventional cases. This "big-picture" version can be programmed as

```
If a = 0 Then
   'weird cases
Else
   'quadratic formula
End If
```

Next, we refine the code to handle the "weird" cases:

```
'weird cases
If b <> 0 Then
   'single root
   r1 = -c / b
Else
   'trivial solution
   MsgBox "Trivial solution. Reenter data"
End If
```

Now we can refine the code further to handle the conventional cases with the quadratic formula:

```
'quadratic formula
d = b ^ 2 - 4 * a * c
If d >= 0 Then
   'real roots
   r1 = (-b + Sqr(d)) / (2 * a)
   r2 = (-b - Sqr(d)) / (2 * a)
Else
   'complex roots
   r1 = -b / (2 * a)
   r2 = r1
   i1 = Sqr(Abs(d)) / (2 * a)
   i2 = -i1
End If
```

We can then merely substitute these blocks back into the simple "big-picture" framework to give the final result:

```
If a = 0 Then
   'weird cases
   If b <> 0 Then
      'single root
      r1 = -c / b
   Else
      'trivial solution
      MsgBox "Trivial solution. Reenter data"
   End If
Else
```

```
'quadratic formula
 d = b ^ 2 - 4 * a * c
 If d >= 0 Then
    'real roots
    r1 = (-b + Sqr(d)) / (2 * a)
    r2 = (-b - Sqr(d)) / (2 * a)
 Else
    'complex roots
        r1 = -b / (2 * a)
        r2 = r1
        i1 = Sqr(Abs(d)) / (2 * a)
        i2 = -i1
    End If
End If
```

The shading shows how indentation helps to make the underlying logical structure of the program clear. Notice how "modular" the structures are. The flowchart representation in Figure 11.8 exhibits the same structure.

11.7 COMPOUND LOGICAL EXPRESSIONS

VBA allows the testing of more than one logical condition by employing logical operators, some of which are as follows:

- **And (Conjunction).** Used to perform the logical conjunction of two expressions:

$$result = expression_1 \text{ And } expression_2$$

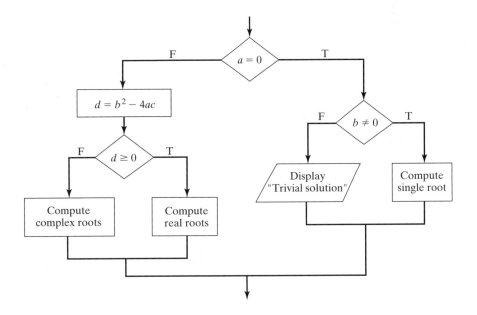

Figure 11.8. A flowchart for determining the roots of the quadratic equation with the use of nested If/Then/Else statements.

If both *expressions* evaluate to True, *result* is True. If either *expression* evaluates to False, *result* is False.

- **Or (Disjunction, or Inclusive Or).** Used to perform the logical disjunction of two expressions:

$$result = expression_1 \text{ Or } expression_2$$

If either or both of *expression₁* and *expression₂* evaluate to True, *result* is True.

- **Not (Logical Complement).** Used to perform logical negation on an expression:

$$result = \text{Not } expression$$

If *expression* is True, *result* is False. Conversely, if *expression* is False, *result* is True.

Table 11-2 summarizes all possible outcomes for each of these operators, as well as for the other available logical operators in VBA.

TABLE 11-2 Truth table summarizing possible outcomes involving all logical operators employed in VBA. The order of priority of the operators is shown at the top of the table.

		Highest priority					Lowest priority
x	y	Not x	x And y	x Or y	x Xor y	x Eqv y	x Imp y
T	T	F	T	T	F	T	T
T	F	F	F	T	T	F	F
F	T	T	F	T	T	F	T
F	F	T	F	F	F	T	T

As with arithmetic operators, there is an order of priority for evaluating logical operators. (See Table 11-3.)

TABLE 11-3 Summary of order of priority for evaluating mathematical, relational, and logical operators in VBA.

TYPE	OPERATOR	PRIORITY
ARITHMETIC	Parenthesis, ()	Highest
	Exponentiation, ^	
	Negation, -	
	Multiplication, *, and Division, /	
	Addition, +, and Subtraction, -	
RELATIONAL	=, <>, <, >, <=, >=	
LOGICAL	Not	
	And	
	Or	Lowest
	Left ⟶ Right	

Let's investigate how the computer employs the priorities from Table 11-3 to evaluate a *logical expression*. If a = -1, b = 2, x = 1, and y = "b", is the following expression true or false?

```
a * b > 0 And b = 2 And x > 7 Or Not y > "d"
```

To make the expression easier to evaluate, substitute the values for the variables:

```
-1 * 2 > 0 And 2 = 2 And 1 > 7 Or Not "b" > "d"
```

The first thing that VBA does is to evaluate arithmetic expressions. In this example, there is only one: -1 * 2,

```
-2 > 0 And 2 = 2 And 1 > 7 Or Not "b" > "d"
```

Next, VBA evaluates all the relational expressions:

```
F And T And F Or Not F
```

Now the logical operators are evaluated in order of priority. Since Not has highest priority, the last expression (Not F) is evaluated first, giving

```
F And T And F Or T
```

The And operator is evaluated next. Because it occurs twice, the left-to-right rule is applied, and the first expression (F And T) is evaluated:

```
F And F Or T
```

The And operator again has highest priority, so we have

```
F Or T
```

Finally, the Or is evaluated as true. The entire process is depicted in Figure 11.9.

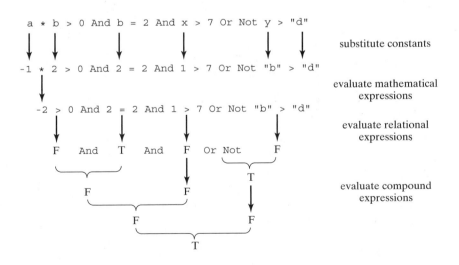

Figure 11.9.   A step-by-step evaluation of a complex decision.

11.7.1 Logical Complements and DeMorgan's Theorem

Clearly the opposite of equality (=) is inequality (<>). Such opposites are called *logical complements*. The complements of the logical operators are summarized in Table 11-4.

TABLE 11-4 Complements for the Relational Operators

OPERATOR	COMPLEMENT	IDENTIFY
=	<>	a = b is equivalent to NOT (a <> b)
<	>=	a < b is equivalent to NOT (a >= b)
>	<=	a > b is equivalent to NOT (a <= b)
<=	>	a <= b is equivalent to NOT (a > b)
>=	<	a >= b is equivalent to NOT (a < b)
<>	=	a <> b is equivalent to NOT (a = b)

Note that in most cases, it is clearer and more convenient to use the complement of a relational operator than to employ the Not. On the other hand, there will be other instances where the Not will be desirable.

De Morgan's theorem is often helpful in clarifying logical expressions. It amounts to the following identities

```
Not x And Not Y ≡ Not (x or y)
Not x Or Not y ≡ Not (x And y)
```

A simple example can serve to illustrate the utility of logical complements and De Morgan's theorem. Suppose that it is safe to run a chemical process if the following compound condition is true

```
Not (Temp > 300 Or press > 100)
```

The condition can be stated in words as: The chemical process is safe if it is not true that the temperature is greater than 300 K or that the pressure is greater than 100 atm. Applying De Morgan's theorem yields the following equivalent expression

```
Not Temp > 300 And Not Press > 100
```

In other words, an alternative (and I think clearer) way of expressing of logic is to say that the process is safe if the temperature is not greater than 300 and the pressure is not greater than 100

Logical complements can be applied to simplify the statement further as in

```
Temp <= 300 And Press <= 100
```

That is, the process is safe if the temperature is less than or equal to 300 and the pressure is less than or equal to 100.

KEY TERMS

Control structures
De Morgan's theorem
Decisions
Flowchart
GoTo statement
If/Then/Else structure
If/Then/Elself structure

Kangaroo codes
Logical complements
Logical expression
Loops
Nesting
Repetition
Select Case structure

Selection
Single-line If statement
Spaghetti codes
Structured programming
Top-down design

Problems

1. What will be displayed when the Sub procedure that follows is run, true or false? Show all the steps in your evaluation, as in Figure 11.9.

```
Option Explicit
Sub test()
Dim x As Double, z As Double
Dim a As String, b As String
x = 7.
z = 6.
a = "b"
b = "a"
If Not z > 4 * Atn(1) Or rrr(x) < z Or x > 7 And a > b Then
  MsgBox "true"
Else
  MsgBox "false"
End If
End Sub
Function rrr(x)
  rrr = -x
End Function
```

2. Consider the following code:

```
Option Explicit
Dim r As Double, s As Double, t As Double
Dim k As String, m As String
r = 2
s = 4
t = 4
m = "s"
k = "t"
```

Are the expressions that follow true or false? Show all the steps in making your evaluation, as in Figure 11.9.

(*a*) (Sqr(s) >= r Or m < k) And NOT s * r ^ 2 <= t ^ 2
(*b*) Sqr(s) >= r Or m < k And NOT s * r ^ 2 <= t ^ 2

3. What message will be displayed when the Sub procedure that follows is run? Show all the steps in your evaluation, as in Figure 11.9.

```
Option Explicit
Sub Test()
Dim w As Double, x As Double, y As Double
Dim cra As String, dza As String
Dim Cond As Boolean
w = -7#
x = 3.14
y = Int(x)
cra = "dzz"
dza = "cra"
Cond = Not "dra" >= cra And (x <> y Or Abs(w) > w) And -2 ^ 3 > w
If Cond Then
  MsgBox Cond
Else
```

```
        MsgBox Cond
    End If
End Sub
```

4. Write a well-structured VBA procedure that returns values of x and y in accordance with the flowchart shown in Figure 11.10.

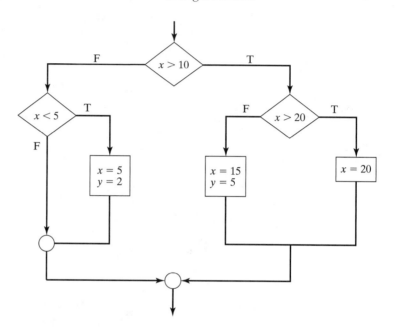

Figure 11.10.

5. What values of x are represented by the Else clause of the following Select Case?

```
Select Case a
  Case Is < 0
    x = 0
  Case Is < 50
    x = 50
  Case Is < 100
    x = 100
  Case Else
    x = 200
End Select
```

6. It is relatively straightforward to compute Cartesian coordinates (x, y) on the basis of polar coordinates (r, θ). The reverse process, however, is not so simple. The radius can be computed by the following formula:

$$r = \sqrt{x^2 + y^2}$$

(11-2)

If the coordinates lie in the first or fourth quadrant (that is, if $x > 0$), then the following simple formula can be used to compute θ:

$$\theta = \tan^{-1}\left(\frac{y}{x}\right)$$

(11-3)

The difficulty arises with the other two quadrants and when $x = 0$. The following table summarizes the possibilities:

x	y	θ
<0	>0	$\tan^{-1}\left(\dfrac{y}{x}\right)+\pi$
<0	<0	$\tan^{-1}\left(\dfrac{y}{x}\right)+\pi$
<0	$=0$	π
$=0$	>0	$\dfrac{\pi}{2}$
$=0$	<0	$-\dfrac{\pi}{2}$
$=0$	$=0$	π

Write a well-structured Sub procedure to compute (r, θ), given (x, y). Express the final results for θ in degrees. The following is the start of the problem:

```
Sub Polar(x, y, r, th)
Dim x as Double, y As Double, r as Double, th As Double
.
.
.
End Sub
```

7. Identify and correct the five syntax errors in the following code:

```
Option Explicit
Sub CritArea()
Dim r As Variant, critmsg As String
Dim A As Double
critmsg = Explosion
r = InputBox "Enter radius (m):"
pi = 3.141593
A = ((pi) * (r ^ (2)))
If A > 300 Then MsgBox(critmsg, , "Pressure exceeded")
End If
End Sub
```

8. Prove that De Morgan's theorem holds for any number of terms.

```
Not (A And B And... And Z) ≡ Not A Or Not B Or... Or Not Z
Not (A Or B Or... Or Z) ≡ Not A And Not B And... And Not Z
```

Hint: prove it for three terms and cluster two of the options,

```
Not ((A And B) And C) ≡ Not A Or Not B Or Not C
```

9. Suppose that a consulting engineer has the task of designing a pollution alert system for a swimming beach. They come up with the following code to trigger an alert

```
If Not (Not W And (V Or R)) Then
  MsgBox "Safe to swim"
Else
  MsgBox "Swimming advisory"
End If
```

where W is true in the winter when the beach is closed, V is true if there was a bacterial violation at the beach on the previous day, and R is true if it rained the previous day.

(*a*) Apply De Morgan's theorem and logical complements to simplify the logical condition.

(*b*) Negate (that is, apply a Not) to your result from part (*a*) to reverse the sense of the If statement. That is, if the new condition is true then display a swimming advisory.

```
If new condition Then
  MsgBox "Swimming advisory"
Else
  MsgBox "Safe to swim"
End If
```

Apply De Morgan's theorem and logical complements to simplify the new condition.

12

Structured Programming: Loops

Suppose that you want to execute a statement or a group of statements many times. One simple way of accomplishing this is to write the set of statements over and over again. For example, a repetitive version of a simple program that adds two numbers is

```
Option Explicit
Sub Add()
Dim a As Double, b As Double
a = InputBox("Enter first number: ")
b = InputBox("Enter second number: ")
MsgBox "The sum is " & a + b
a = InputBox("Enter first number: ")
b = InputBox("Enter second number: ")
MsgBox "The sum is " & a + b
a = InputBox("Enter first number: ")
b = InputBox("Enter second number: ")
  .
  .
  .
End Sub
```

SECTIONS

- 12.1 Decision Loops (Do/if Exit)
- 12.2 Count-controlled Loops
- 12.3 Nesting of Loops and Decisions
- 12.4 Recursion

OBJECTIVES

After reading this chapter, you should able to

- Recognize the difference between decision and count-controlled loops.
- Understand how the Do/If Exit loop operates with emphasis on the placement of the If/Exit statement.
- Understand how the For/Next loop operates for different start, finish and step values.
- Understand how nested loops and nested loops and decisions are structured.
- Understand recursion and how a recursive process is terminated.

Because we have to repeat the statements, such a sequential approach is obviously inefficient.

A much more concise alternative can be developed using the VBA *Do/Loop structure*:

```
Do
   [statements]
Loop
```

The loop starts at the Do. It then executes the statements down to the Loop statement, which transfers control back to the Do, and the statements are executed again.

The Do/Loop can be used in the simple addition program as follows:

```
Option Explicit
Sub Add()
Dim a As Double, b As Double
Do
  a = InputBox("Enter first number: ")
  b = InputBox("Enter second number: ")
  MsgBox "The sum is " & a + b
Loop
End Sub
```

Thus, the algorithm is repeated over and over again.

An obvious flaw of this application is that it never ends! A loop that never ends is referred to as an *infinite loop*. To overcome this problem, provisions must be made so that the loop is exited after a finite number of repetitions. Two different approaches are employed to terminate loops. *Decision loops* are terminated on the basis of the state of a logical expression (in other words, an expression that is either true or false). In this sense, decision loops are related to the decision constructs discussed in the previous chapter. Because such loops involve a decision, they may repeat a different number of times on every execution. In contrast, *count-controlled loops* are preset to repeat a fixed number of times.

12.1 DECISION LOOPS (DO/IF EXIT)

As the name Do/If Exit implies, decision loops terminate if a condition is true. The general representation is

```
Do
   [statements]
   If condition Then Exit Do
   [statements]
Loop
```

where *condition* is a logical condition that tests True or False. Thus, a *single-line If statement* is used to exit the loop if the condition tests true. Note that, as shown, the exit can be placed in the middle of the loop (that is, with statements before and after it). Such a structure is called a *mid-test loop*.

If the problem required it, we could place the exit at the very beginning to create a *pretest loop*. An example is

```
Do
   If x < 0 Then Exit Do
   x = x - 5
Loop
```

Notice how 5 is subtracted from x on each iteration. This subtraction represents a mechanism that allows the loop to terminate eventually. Every decision loop must have such a mechanism. Otherwise it would repeat *ad infinitum*.

Alternatively, we could place the If Exit at the very end and create a *posttest loop*:

```
Do
  x = x - 5
  If x < 0 Then Exit Do
Loop
```

The flowchart representation of the Do/If Exit loop is shown in Figure 12.1. Although the loop is the midtest version, the flowchart should make it clear that, in fact, all three structures are really the same. That is, where we put the exit (at the beginning, in the middle, or at the end) dictates whether we have a pre-, mid- or posttest.[1]

12.2   COUNT-CONTROLLED LOOPS

Suppose you want to perform a specific number of repetitions, or iterations, of a loop. One way to do this with a Do/If Exit construct described in the previous section is depicted in the flowchart and program fragment shown in Figure 12.2.

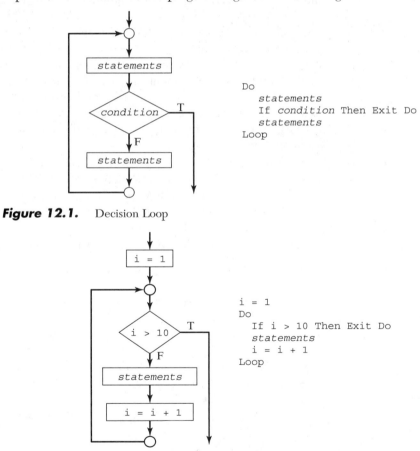

```
Do
    statements
    If condition Then Exit Do
    statements
Loop
```

Figure 12.1.   Decision Loop

```
i = 1
Do
    If i > 10 Then Exit Do
    statements
    i = i + 1
Loop
```

Figure 12.2.   Using a Do/If Exit structure to loop a prespecified number of times.

---

[1] It is this simplicity that led the computer scientists who developed Fortran 90 to favor the Do/If Exit construct over other forms of the decision loop (like the Do While or Do Until).

This loop is designed to repeat 10 times. The variable i is the counter that keeps track of the number of iterations. If i is *less than or equal* to 10, an iteration is performed. On each pass, i is incremented by 1. After the 10th iteration, i will become 11. Therefore, the If statement will test true, and the loop will terminate.

Although the Do/If Exit loop is certainly a feasible option for performing a specified number of iterations, such looping operations are so common that a special set of statements is available in VBA for accomplishing the same objective in a more efficient manner. Called the *For/Next loop*, this set of statements has the general format

```
For counter = start To finish [Step increment]
    [statements]
    [Exit For]
    [statements]
Next [counter]
```

where *counter* is a numeric variable used as a loop counter, *start* is the initial value of *counter*, *finish* is the final value of *counter*, *increment* is the amount *counter* is changed each time the loop is executed (If it is not specified, *increment* defaults to 1), and statements are one or more statements between For and Next that are executed the specified number of times.

The For/Next loop operates as follows: The variable *counter* is set at an initial value, *start*. The program then compares *counter* with the desired final value, *finish*. If *counter* is less than or equal to *finish*, the program executes the body of the loop. When the Next statement that marks the end of the loop is reached, *counter* is increased by *increment*, and the program loops back to the For statement. The process continues until *counter* becomes greater than *finish*. At this point, the loop terminates, and the program skips down to the line immediately following the loop's terminus, Next *counter*.

Thus, the For/Next loop works identically to the Do/If Exit loop in Figure 12.2. However, Figure 12.3 illustrates the superiority of the For/Next.

If an Exit For statement is encountered, the loop will terminate, and the program moves to the line immediately following the Next statement. Any number of Exit For statements may be placed anywhere in the loop as an alternative way of exiting. Exit For is often used in conjunction with a decision, as for example, in

```
If condition Then Exit For
```

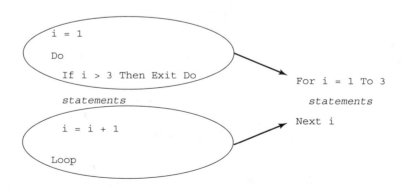

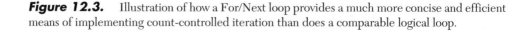

Figure 12.3. Illustration of how a For/Next loop provides a much more concise and efficient means of implementing count-controlled iteration than does a comparable logical loop.

If an *increment* of 1 is desired (as is often the case), the Step part of the For statement may be dropped. For example, when the code

```
For i = 1 To 5
   MsgBox i
Next i
```

executes, the computer would display, in succession, 1, 2, 3, 4, and 5. In other words, the default *increment* is 1.

The size of *increment* can be changed from the default of 1 to any other numeric value. It does not have to be an integer, nor does it have to be positive. For example, *increment* sizes of –5, 0.5, or 60 are all acceptable.

If a negative *increment* is used, the loop will "count down" in reverse. In such cases, the loop's logic is reversed. Thus, *finish* must be less than or equal to *start*, and the loop terminates when *counter* is less than *finish*. For example, when

```
For j = 10 To 1 Step -1
   MsgBox j
Next j
```

executes, the computer displays the classic "countdown" sequence: 10, 9, 8, 7, 6, 5, 4, 3, 2, 1.

Another subtlety of the way For/Next loops operate is illustrated by the code

```
For count = 2 To 14 Step 4
   MsgBox count
Next count
Msgbox "After the loop:"
Msgbox count
```

The resulting display will be

```
2
6
10
14
After the loop:
18
```

Notice that, upon exit from the loop, count has been incremented by 4 beyond *finish*, the limit of the loop. This is a direct result of the way the loop operates.

Here's another example, but counting backwards:

```
For j = 20 To -5 Step -6
   MsgBox j
Next j
Msgbox "After the loop:"
Msgbox j
```

The resulting display will be

```
20
14
8
2
-4
After the loop:
-10
```

The flowchart for a For/Next loop is shown in Figure 12.4.

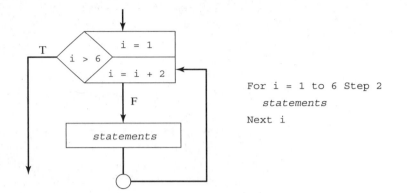

```
For i = 1 to 6 Step 2
    statements
Next i
```

Figure 12.4. Flowchart representation of the For/Next loop.

12.3 NESTING OF LOOPS AND DECISIONS

Loops may be enclosed completely within other loops. This arrangement, called *nesting*, is valid only if it follows the rule that a For/Next loop contains either the For or the Next part of another loop, it must contain both of them. Figure 12.5 presents some correct and incorrect versions of nesting. Notice how indentation is used to delineate the extent of the loops.

An example of nesting is provided by the code

```
For i = 2 To 4 Step 2
  For j = 3 To 9 Step 5
    MsgBox i & " " & j
  Next j
Next i
MsgBox "After the loop: i = " & i & "; j = " & j
```

Let's examine how such code executes. The first For statement sets i to 2, and the second sets j to 3. Therefore, the first message box will display 2 and 3. Then, the Next j statement increments j by 5, so that now j = 8. Because j does not exceed the limit (9), the second loop executes again, and values of 2 and 8 are displayed. The Next j statement again increments j to give j = 13. Because this is greater than the loop's limit (9), the second loop terminates.

At this point, the Next i statement increments i by 2 to give i = 4. Because i does not exceed the first loop's limit (4), the second loop starts up again and resets j to 3. The next message box displays 4 and 3. Then, the Next j statement increments j by 5, so that j = 8. The next message box displays 4 and 8. The Next j again increments j to give j = 13. Because this is greater than the loop's limit (9), the second loop terminates.

At this point, the Next i statement increments i by 2 to give i = 6. Because this value exceed the first loop's limit of 4, the first loop terminates. Consequently, the final message box displays the last values of i and j: 6 and 13, respectively. To summarize, the values displayed would be as follows:

```
i   j
2   3
2   8
4   3
4   8
After the loop:
6   13
```

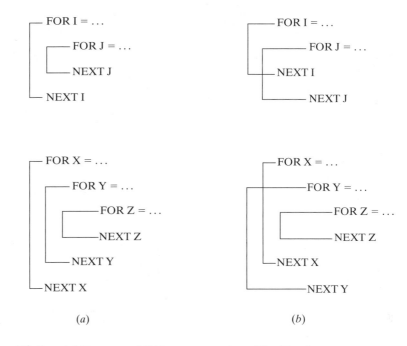

```
 ┌── FOR I = …                         ┌── FOR I = …
 │     ┌── FOR J = …                   │     ┌── FOR J = …
 │     └── NEXT J                      └── NEXT I
 └── NEXT I                                  └── NEXT J


 ┌── FOR X = …                         ┌── FOR X = …
 │     ┌── FOR Y = …                   │     ┌── FOR Y = …
 │     │     ┌── FOR Z = …             │     │     ┌── FOR Z = …
 │     │     └── NEXT Z                │     │     └── NEXT Z
 │     └── NEXT Y                      └── NEXT X
 └── NEXT X                                  └── NEXT Y
```

(*a*)   (*b*)

Figure 12.5.   (*a*) Correct and (*b*) incorrect nesting of For/Next loops.

12.4 RECURSION

Recursion is a powerful problem-solving tool that is available in certain computer languages, such as VBA. A *recursive process* is a process that calls itself (Figure 12.6).

Figure 12.6.   Graphical depiction of a recursive process.

The factorial calculation is a good example of mathematical recursion. For example, the quantity 5! is conventionally calculated as

$$5! = 5 \times 4 \times 3 \times 2 \times 1$$

However, it can also be recast as a recursive sequence:

$$5! = 5 \cdot 4!$$
$$4! = 4 \cdot 3!$$
$$3! = 3 \cdot 2!$$
$$2! = 2 \cdot 1!$$
$$1! = 1 \cdot 0!$$

The next Hands-on Exercise illustrates how this pattern can be expressed concisely by utilizing VBA's ability to exploit recursion.

12.4.1 Hands-on Exercise: Nonrecursive and Recursive Factorial Functions

In this exercise, we will develop both nonrecursive and recursive functions to compute factorials.

STEP 1: Start Excel, and enter the following information on Sheet1:

	A	B	C	D
1	Recursive Factorial Function			
2				
3	n	n! (nonrecursive)	n! (recursive)	
4	0			
5	1			
6	2			
7	3			
8	4			
9	5			
10	6			
11	7			
12	8			
13	9			
14	10			
15				

STEP 2: First, let's develop a function that implements factorials without recursion. Go to the VBE, insert a module, and type in the following code:

```
Function Factorial(n)
Dim i As Integer
Factorial = 1
For i = 1 To n
  Factorial = Factorial * i
Next i
End Function
```

Suppose that n = 3. Before the loop is entered, `Factorial` is initialized to 1. For the first iteration of the loop (i = 1), `Factorial` is computed as

```
Factorial = 1 * 1 = 1
```

On the second iteration ($i = 2$),

```
Factorial = 1 * 2 = 2
```

On the final iteration ($i = 3$),

```
Factorial = 2 * 3 = 6
```

At this point, the loop terminates, and the function returns the correct value for $3! = 1 \times 2 \times 3 = 6$. Notice that for 0!, the loop would never execute, and the correct factorial of 0! = 1 is returned.

Go back to the worksheet and enter the function into cell B4:

```
=Factorial(A4)
```

As expected, a 1 should appear in cell B4. Copy the formula to cells B5:B14, and the correct values for the other factorials should be displayed.

STEP 3: Now let's develop an alternative factorial function that exploits recursion. Directly below the nonrecursive function, type in the following code:

```
Function FactRecurs(n)
If n > 0 Then
  FactRecurs = n * FactRecurs(n - 1)
Else
  FactRecurs = 1
End If
End Function
```

Again, suppose that n = 3. When the function is initially invoked, the If statement will test True, and FactRecurs will be computed as

```
FactRecurs = 3 * FactRecurs(2)
```

Notice that this results in FactRecurs calling itself recursively, but this time with an argument of 2. In this case, the If statement will again test True, and FactRecurs will be computed as

```
FactRecurs = 2 * FactRecurs(1)
```

Thus, FactRecurs calls itself again, but now with an argument of 1. Again, the If statement will test True, and FactRecurs will be computed as

```
FactRecurs = 1 * FactRecurs(0)
```

Because n = 0, the If statement will test False, and the Else clause will be implemented as

```
FactRecurs = 1
```

Now, because this assignment statement does not invoke another function, the function terminates naturally and returns a value of 1 to the previous invocation (FactRecurs(1)). Thus,

```
FactRecurs = 2 * FactRecurs(1) = 2 * 1 = 2
```

The process is repeated as the value is returned to the initial invocation,

```
FactRecurs = 3 * FactRecurs(2) = 3 * 2 = 6
```

and the function terminates completely and returns a value of 6. At the end of the process, n will hold a value of 6 ($3! = 3 \times 2 \times 1$).

STEP 4: Go back to the worksheet, and enter the following formula into cell C4:

```
=FactRecurs(A4)
```

A 1 should appear in cell B4. Now copy the formula to cells B5:B14, and the correct values for the other factorials should be displayed. The final worksheet looks like this:

	A	B	C	D
	C14		ƒx =factrecurs(A14)	
1	Factorial Functions			
2				
3	n	n! (nonrecursive)	n! (recursive)	
4	0	1	1	
5	1	1	1	
6	2	2	2	
7	3	6	6	
8	4	24	24	
9	5	120	120	
10	6	720	720	
11	7	5040	5040	
12	8	40320	40320	
13	9	362880	362880	
14	10	3628800	3628800	
15				

Note that a recursive process must always have a terminating condition. Otherwise, it would go on forever. In the case of factorials, the condition arises naturally from the fact that 0! = 1. Consequently, when 0! is called, the IF statement shifts to an assignment statement rather than another invocation of the function, thereby allowing the process to terminate.

KEY TERMS

Count-controlled loop	If/Exit statement	Posttest loop
Decision loop	Infinite loop	Pretest loop
Do/Loop structure	Mid-test loop	Recursion
For/Next loop	Nesting	Recursive process

Problems

1. What will be displayed when the following code is run?

```
(a) For i = 4 To -1 Step -3
      For j = -1 to 1
        MsgBox i * j
      Next j
    Next i
    Msgbox "After the loop:"
    Msgbox i * j
```

(*b*)
```
j = 3
Do
   If j > 8 Then Exit Do
   For i = 7 To 4 Step -2
     MsgBox i & " " & j
   Next i
   j = j + 4
Loop
MsgBox i & " " & j
```

(*c*)
```
For i = 7 To 4 Step -2
   For j = -2 To 5 Step 5
     MsgBox i + j
   Next j
   MsgBox i + j
Next i
```

(*d*)
```
For i = -6 To -14 Step -8
   For j = 2 To 5 Step 4
     MsgBox i & " " & j
   Next j
   MsgBox i & " " & j
Next i
MsgBox i & " " & j
```

2. Write a well-structured VBA function procedure, x, that returns a value computed in accordance with the following flowchart:

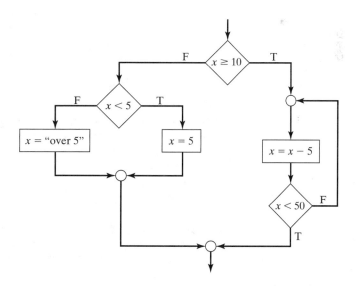

3. Write a well-structured VBA Sub procedure, *xycalc*, that returns values of the integers x and y in accordance wih the following flowchart:

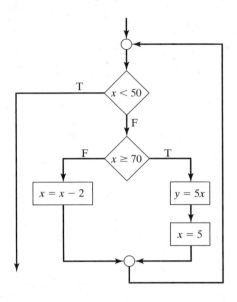

4.   The infinite series for the cosine of x is

$$\cos x = \sum_{i=0}^{n} (-1)^i \frac{x^{2i}}{(2i)!}$$

or, in expanded form,

$$\cos x = \frac{x^0}{0!} - \frac{x^2}{2!} + \frac{x^4}{4!} - \frac{x^6}{6!} + \dots$$

Write a Sub procedure, `cosine`, that uses this formula to calculate the value of the cosine of x, given x and the number of terms, n. Use a separate procedure, `Fac`, to calculate the factorial of x. Do not have the Sub procedure do any input or output. That is, just do the calculation. Here is the calling program:

```
Option Explicit
Sub CosEvaluate()
Dim n As Integer
Dim x As Double, c As Double
x = InputBox("Enter value of x:")
n = InputBox("Enter number of evaluations:")
Call Cosine(x, n, c)
MsgBox c
End Sub
```

5.   Although it can be implemented with the exponentiation operator (^), integer exponentiation is an excellent example of a recursive function. Exponentiation can be expressed recursively as

$$x^0 = 1$$
$$x^1 = x \cdot x^0$$
$$x^2 = x \cdot x^1$$
$$x^3 = x \cdot x^2$$
.
.
.
$$x^n = x \cdot x^{n-1}$$

Develop a recursive function procedure that implements this algorithm. Call the procedure Xpower.

6. The "golden ratio" is related to an important mathematical sequence known as the Fibonacci numbers, which are

$$0, 1, 1, 2, 3, 5, 8, 13, 21, 34, \ldots$$

In other words, each number after the first two is the sum of the preceding two. An interesting property of the Fibonacci sequence relates to the ratio of consecutive numbers in the sequence; that is, $0/1 = 0$, $1/1 = 1$, $1/2 = 0.5$, $2/3 = 0.667$, $3/5 = 0.6$, $5/8 = 0.625$, and so on. If the series is carried out far enough, the ratio approaches the golden ratio

$$\frac{\sqrt{5} - 1}{2} = 0.618033988749895\ldots$$

The Fibonacci sequence can be expressed recursively as

$$f(0) = 0$$
$$f(1) = 1$$
$$f(2) = f(1) + f(0)$$
$$f(3) = f(2) + f(1)$$
.
.
.
$$f(3) = f(2) + f(1)$$

Develop a recursive function procedure to implement this algorithm. Call the procedure Fibonacci(n). Test it by computing the golden ratio.

7. Compound interest is computed by

$$A_n = (1 + i)^n \cdot A_0 \tag{12-1}$$

where A_0 is the original amount that was borrowed, A_n is the amount owed after n periods, and i is the fractional rate of interest. It can also be represented by the recursive process

$$A_0 = A_0$$
$$A_1 = (1+i) \cdot A_0$$
$$A_2 = (1+i) \cdot A_1$$
$$\cdot$$
$$\cdot$$
$$\cdot$$
$$A_n = (1+i) \cdot A_{n-1}$$

which can be expressed concisely by the general formula

$$A_n = (1+i) \cdot A_{n-1}$$

Use a recursive function to program the process. Employ Eq. 12-1 to verify that your procedure yields correct results.

8.   Write a recursive function that computes the sum of the integers

$$1, 2, 3, \ldots, n$$

Specify the argument as n.

13

Data Structures: Arrays and Records

Just as structured programming constructs make computer code easier to understand, data can also be organized to make its use more efficient. Such organization is called *data structuring*.

The most fundamental way to structure data is by declaring variable types using Option Explicit and Dim, Const and Public statements. This chapter covers two other features that foster more efficient and succinct organization of information: arrays and records.

An array is a collection of values that are referenced by a single variable name. The individual values are then accessed with subscripts. Whereas all the values of an array must be of the same variable type, records allow you to store different types using a single variable name. This provides a useful vehicle for storing and manipulating databases consisting of different types of information. In the present chapter, we will use information from the periodic table to illustrate the utility of records.

SECTIONS

- 13.1 Arrays
- 13.2 Records

OBJECTIVES

After reading this chapter, you should be able to

- Understand that arrays are really just subscripted variables.
- Use subscripts to access particular values in an array.
- Dimension and specify the type of an array.
- Store multi-dimensional data in arrays.
- Specify an array's lower bound.
- Pass arrays to procedures.
- Redimension a dynamic array.
- Save and access a collection of different type data in a record.
- Dimension and define record data types.
- Pass records to procedures.

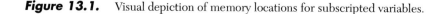

13.1   ARRAYS

Subscripted variables are commonplace in algebra, as, for example, in the equation

$$y = 3x_1 + 4x_2 - 7x_3$$

The counterpart in VBA is called an *array*. Instead of subscripts, parentheses are used, as in the assignment statement

```
y = 3 * x(1) + 4 * x(2) - 7 * x(3)
```

In VBA, you are required to declare arrays. As with simple variable typing, this is done with the Dim statement. The general syntax is

```
Dim aname(sbs) [As type] [, varname(sbs) [As type]] . . .
```

where *aname* is the array's name, *sbs* denotes the subscripts, and *type* is the data type.

In the algebraic example, we could dimension the array *x* as

```
Dim x(4) as Double
```

As depicted in Figure 13.1, this declaration sets aside five memory locations for the subscripted variable *x* (subscripts 0 through 4). It also serves the purpose of specifying the data type of the variable.

As constants are assigned to the elements of the array, they will be stored in the designated memory locations. Thereafter, the individual values can be accessed by the name with the particular subscript. This is what occurs when the equation is implemented as in Figure 13.1 The result of the calculation would be displayed in the following message box:

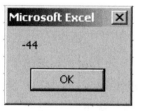

```
Option Explicit
Sub Example ()
Dim i As Integer
Dim x (4) As Double, y As Double
For i = 1 To 3
  x(i) = i * i
Next i
y = 3 * x(1) + 4 * x(2) - 7 * x(3)
MsgBox y
End Sub
```

Figure 13.1.   Visual depiction of memory locations for subscripted variables.

If you do not make the dimension of the array large enough, you will get an error message. However, as in Figure 13.1, you will often make the dimension larger than necessary in anticipation of the possibility that you eventually will use the code for problems with a greater number of array elements. The maximum size of an array varies with your operating system and how much memory is available. Using an array that exceeds the amount of RAM on your system is slower, because the data must be read from and written to disk.

Arrays are used in many contexts in engineering. Figure 13.2 shows an uninsulated metal bar fixed between two walls. Because of heat transfer processes such as conduction and radiation, the resulting temperature is as displayed in the plot below the rod.

Engineers typically measure the temperature at points along the rod, as summarized in the following table:

x	0	2.5	5	7.5	10
T	40	175	245	255	200

These values could be stored in the computer as a simple variable. The following code uses that approach and also converts the Celsius temperatures to Fahrenheit:

```
Option Explicit
Sub TempSimp()
Dim Tc0 As Double, Tc1 As Double, Tc2 As Double
Dim Tc3 As Double, Tc4 As Double
Dim Tf0 As Double, Tf1 As Double, Tf2 As Double
Dim Tf3 As Double, Tf4 As Double
Tc0 = 40: Tc1 = 175: Tc2 = 245: Tc3 = 255: Tc4 = 200
Tf0 = 9 / 5 * Tc0 + 32
Tf1 = 9 / 5 * Tc1 + 32
```

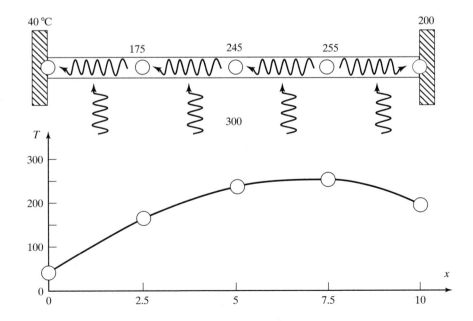

Figure 13.2. The temperature distribution along a heated rod.

```
Tf2 = 9 / 5 * Tc2 + 32
Tf3 = 9 / 5 * Tc3 + 32
Tf4 = 9 / 5 * Tc4 + 32
End Sub
```

Because of all the duplication, this is a highly inefficient way to solve the problem. In contrast, using arrays is much more efficient:

```
Option Explicit
Sub TempArray()
Dim i As Integer, n As Integer
Dim Tc(100) As Double, TF(100) As Double
n = 4
Tc(0) = 40: Tc(1) = 175: Tc(2) = 245: Tc(3) = 255: Tc(4) = 200
For i = 0 To n
  TF(i) = 9 / 5 * Tc(i) + 32
Next i
End Sub
```

Notice that, with the loop counter as the subscript, the For/Next loop represents the conversion process in just three lines. The power of loops and arrays is explored in more detail in the next exercise.

13.1.1 Hands-on Exercise: Loops and Arrays

One area where the combination of loops and arrays shines is that of making data input and output more efficient.

STEP 1: Open a new workbook and save it as *LoopArray.xls*. Enter the following table of times and temperatures on Sheet1:

	A	B
1		
2		
3	Time (hr)	Temperature (decC)
4	0	4
5	1	4.2
6	3	5
7	5	7
8	6	8
9	9	10
10	12	5
11	15	3.5

A heavy-handed way to enter such data would be with code like the following:

```
Option Explicit
Sub InefficientInput()
Dim t(100) As Double, Temp(100) As Double
Sheets("Sheet1").Select
Range("a4").Select
'input the data
t(1) = ActiveCell.Value
ActiveCell.Offset(0, 1).Select
Temp(1) = ActiveCell.Value
```

```
ActiveCell.Offset(1, -1).Select
t(2) = ActiveCell.Value
ActiveCell.Offset(0, 1).Select
Temp(2) = ActiveCell.Value
ActiveCell.Offset(1, -1).Select
t(3) = ActiveCell.Value
ActiveCell.Offset(0, 1).Select
Temp(3) = ActiveCell.Value
ActiveCell.Offset(1, -1).Select
          .
          .
          .
t(8) = ActiveCell.Value
ActiveCell.Offset(0, 1).Select
Temp(8) = ActiveCell.Value
End Sub
```

Such an approach has several major deficiencies. First, most of the statements are repeated. Thus, to enter all eight pairs of numbers would require 32 lines of code. In addition, suppose that you wanted to use the same code to analyze a larger data set. Then you would have to add more lines to your program. Thus, every time you run the program with a different number of nodes, you would have to add or subtract lines from the code.

STEP 2: Go to the VBE and insert a module. Type in the following statements:

```
Option Explicit
Sub EfficientInput()
Dim i As Integer, nt As Integer
Dim t(100), Temp(100) As Double
          .
          .
          .
End Sub
```

STEP 3: Rather than "wiring" the program to process a specific quantity of values, let's have the program count the number of cells of data. The following code accomplishes this task:

```
'determines the number of data in column A
Sheets("Sheet1").Select
Range("a4").Select
nt = Activecell.Row
Selection.End(xlDown).Select
nt = ActiveCell.Row - nt + 1
```

After positioning the cursor at the top of the column of data, we employ the Row property to determine the row number of the first row of data. This value can be assigned to the variable nt. The Selection.End(xlDown).Select statement, which mimics the *End–Down Arrow* key combination, is used to move the cursor to the end of the column. The quantity of data is then determined by subtracting the number of the top row from that of the bottom row. The resulting number can then be used as the finish value of a For/Next loop to read in the data from the sheet:

```
'input the data
Range("a4").Select
```

```
For i = 1 To nt
  t(i) = ActiveCell.Value
  ActiveCell.Offset(0, 1).Select
  Temp(i) = ActiveCell.Value
  ActiveCell.Offset(1, -1).Select
Next i
```

Notice how the four lines required to move down the table and get the data are written once and then implemented repeatedly through the cycling of the loop. `ActiveCell.Offset` statements are used to move across the columns and down the rows in a systematic fashion. The beauty of this approach is that the same code could be used with no modification for 20,000 times and temperatures on Sheet1!

13.1.2 Multidimensional Arrays

Computer languages like VBA allow for more than one dimension.[1] An example of a two-dimensional array would be a heated plate (Figure 13.3).

Just as with one-dimensional arrays, parentheses are used to hold the subscripts:

```
T(0, 0) = 70 : T(0, 1) = 60 : T(0, 2) = 50 : T(0, 3) = 30
T(1, 0) = 80 : T(1, 1) = 70 : T(1, 2) = 60 : T(1, 3) = 50
T(2, 0) = 90 : T(2, 1) = 80 : T(2, 2) = 70 : T(2, 3) = 60
T(3, 0) = 95 : T(3, 1) = 90 : T(3, 2) = 80 : T(3, 3) = 70
```

Suppose that we wanted to convert these temperatures from Celsius to Fahrenheit. Nested For/Next loops provide an efficient means of doing so:

```
For i = 1 To nr
  For j = 1 to nc
    Tf(i, j) = 9 / 5 * Tc(i, j) + 32
  Next j
Next i
```

Arrays can have up to 60 subscripts. However, engineering problems deal mostly with four dimensions: the three dimensions x, y, and z of Cartesian coordinates and the fourth dimension t of time.

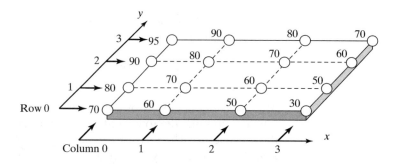

Figure 13.3. A heated plate.

---

[1] One-dimensional and multidimensional arrays are also called *vectors* and *matrices*, respectively.

13.1.3 Changing an Array's Lower Bound

The lower limit of VBA default of 0 on an array derives from the fact that many mathematical constructs employ subscripts starting with 0. For example, an *n*th-order polynomial can be expressed generally as

$$f(x) = a_0 + a_1 x + a_2 x^2 + a_3 x^3 + \ldots + a_n x^n$$

It would be natural to store these coefficients in an array as

```
a(0), a(1), a(2), a(3),...
```

Although the use of 0 as the lower limit follows naturally from mathematics, a different lower limit might follow naturally from the type of data being stored. In such cases, the 0 default can be overridden, as in the code

```
Dim Names(1 TO 10000)
Dim AirTemperature(1954 To 2000)
Dim displacement(-20 To 20)
```

In certain applications, you might like to globally change the lower limit of all arrays to 1. For example, the Fortran language uses 1 as its default lower bound for arrays. Because many useful algorithms are available in Fortran, you might desire to translate a piece of Fortran code into VBA. Setting the lower bound to 1 usually makes the translation easier. The lower bound of all arrays in a module can be set to 1 with the *Option Base statement,* which is placed before the first Sub procedure in the module. The following example shows how the statement is used:

```
Option Explicit
Option Base 1    ' Set default array subscripts to 1.
Sub Test()
Dim x(20) As Double, y(4, 5) As Double
Dim t(0 To 5) As Double ' Overrides default base subscript.
' Use LBound function to test lower bounds of arrays.
MsgBox LBound(x)                        ' Returns 1.
MsgBox LBound(y, 1)                      ' Returns 1.
MsgBox LBound(y, 2)                      ' Returns 1.
MsgBox LBound(t)                         ' Returns 0.
End Sub
```

The function *LBound* returns an array's lower bound. It has the syntax

```
LBound(arrayname[, dimension])
```

where `arrayname` is the name of the array and `dimension` is a whole number indicating which dimension's lower bound is returned. Because of the `Option Base 1` statement, all the arrays except t have lower bounds of 1.

13.1.4 Passing Arrays to Procedures

Arrays can be passed to and from procedures. For example, suppose that we developed a Sub procedure to determine the minimum and maximum values of a one-dimensional array. The `Call` statement could be written as

```
Call MinMax(Temp(), nt, Min, Max)
```

where `Temp()` is the array being analyzed, `nt` is the number of cells of data in the array, and `Min` and `Max` are, respectively, the minimum and maximum values contained in the array. When `MinMax` is called from the procedure in which the array is declared, the array must be referenced with empty parentheses. The parentheses alert VBA that it is dealing with an array, as opposed to a simple variable.

The Sub procedure header would be written as

```
Sub MinMax(x, n, Mn, Mx)
```

Notice that no parentheses are used in the receiving procedure. In addition, different variable names can be used in that procedure.

The following code shows an application to the time–temperature program we developed previously:

```
Option Explicit
Sub Example()
Dim i As Integer, nt As Integer
Dim t(100), Temp(100) As Double
Dim Min As Double, Max As Double
Sheets("Sheet1").Select
Range("a4").Select
'determine the number of data in column A
nt = ActiveCell.Row
Selection.End(xlDown).Select
nt = ActiveCell.Row - nt + 1
'input the data
Range("a4").Select
For i = 1 To nt
  t(i) = ActiveCell.Value
  ActiveCell.Offset(0, 1).Select
  Temp(i) = ActiveCell.Value
  ActiveCell.Offset(1, -1).Select
Next i
Call MinMax(Temp(), nt, Min, Max)
MsgBox "minimum = " & Min & " maximum = " & Max, , _
                    "Temperature"
End Sub
Sub MinMax(x, n, Mn, Mx)
Dim i As Integer
Mn = x(1)
Mx = x(1)
For i = 2 To n
  If x(i) < Mn Then Mn = x(i)
  If x(i) > Mx Then Mx = x(i)
Next i
End Sub
```

When this program is run, the following message box appears:

13.1.5 Hands-on Exercise: The Bubble Sort

The *bubble sort* is an inefficient, but easy-to-understand, method that is just fine for sorting small quantities of data. The idea behind this kind of sort is that one passes down through an array, comparing adjacent pairs and swapping the values if they are out of order. To sort the array completely, one must pass through the array many times. As the passes proceed in an ascending-order sort, the smaller elements in the array appear to rise toward the top like bubbles (Figure 13.4).[2]

Eventually, there will be a pass through the array in which no swaps are required. At that point, the array is sorted. After the first pass, the largest value in the array drops directly to the bottom; consequently, the second pass has to proceed only to the penultimate[3] value, and so on.

STEP 1: Start Excel, go to the VBE, insert a new module, and type in the following Sub procedure:

```
Option Explicit
Sub Test()
Dim i As Long, n As Long
Dim tstart As Double, tfinish As Double
Application.ScreenUpdating = False
n = InputBox("Number of Values = ", "Bubble Sort")
Range("b3").Select
ActiveCell.Value = n
ReDim a(n) As Double, b(n) As Double
'generate n random numbers
For i = 1 To n
  a(i) = Rnd
Next i
'implement bubble sort
Range("b4").Select
tstart = Timer
Call Bubble(n, a(), b())
tfinish = Timer
ActiveCell.Value = tfinish - tstart
'display unsorted and sorted values
```

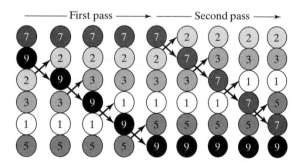

Figure 13.4. Visual depiction of the bubble sort.

---

[2] Conversely, looking at 7 and 9 in the figure, we could alternatively called this type of sort the "sink like a stone" algorithm.

[3] That is, the next-to-last value.

```
Sheets("sheet1").Select
Range("a6:c60005").ClearContents
Range("a6").Select
For i = 1 To n
  ActiveCell.Value = i
  ActiveCell.Offset(0, 1).Select
  ActiveCell.Value = a(i)
  ActiveCell.Offset(0, 1).Select
  ActiveCell.Value = b(i)
  ActiveCell.Offset(1, -2).Select
Next i
Range("l10").Select
Application.ScreenUpdating = True
End Sub
```

A loop is used to assign random numbers between 0 and 1 to the array, which is denoted a(). The number of elements, n, and a() are passed to procedure Bubble, which implements the bubble sort. Notice that we use VBA's *Timer* function to time the sort. Finally, both arrays are displayed on the worksheet. Before proceeding, save the worbook as BubbleSortVBA.xls.

STEP 2: Next let's develop the Bubble Sub procedure. Looking at the pattern in Figure 13.1, we see clearly that the algorithm will consist of two nested loops:

1. An outer loop that iterates through the passes until no switches are made.

2. An inner loop that moves down through the array, making switches where necessary.

Here is the code to implement the bubble sort algorithm:

```
Sub Bubble(n, a, b)
'sorts an array in ascending order
'using the bubble sort
Dim m As Integer, i As Integer
Dim switch As Boolean
Dim dum As Double
For i = 1 To n
  b(i) = a(i)
Next i
m = n - 1
Do                 'loop through passes
  switch = False
  For i = 1 To m 'loop through array
    If b(i) > b(i + 1) Then
      dum = b(i)
      b(i) = b(i + 1)
      b(i + 1) = dum
      switch = True
    End If
  Next i
  If switch = False Then Exit Do
  m = m - 1
Loop
End Sub
```

Notice that the procedure stores the elements of a() in a new array, b(). This is the array that will actually be sorted. We re-store the elements so that we retain the original values in the event that we need them later.

STEP 3: Go back to the workbook and set up a button to run the macro. Debug the program until you have successfully sorted 10 values. Plot the sorted and unsorted values against *n*, and then run the program for 1000 values. The result should look like this:

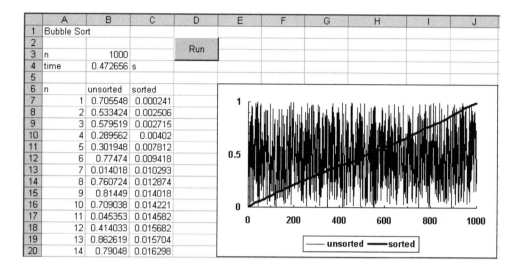

As expected, the unsorted values bounce around randomly between 0 and 1. The sorted values form a nice straight line.

It took about 0.5 s to implement this sort on my computer. Your time will likely be different, depending on the speed of your computer's processor. The execution time for the bubble sort algorithm is proportional to n^2. On my computer, sorting 2000 and 10,000 random numbers took 1.8 and 45.3 s, respectively, which accords with the proportionality.

13.1.6 Dynamic Arrays and the ReDim Statement

To this point, we have used arrays whose size is specified by a Dim statement, such as

```
Dim a(10) as Double
```

This kind of array is called a *fixed-size array*, because once it has been declared, its dimensions cannot be changed.

VBA also has *dynamic arrays* whose size can be changed while a program is running. This is done at the procedure level by declaring the array with empty parentheses, as in

```
Dim a() as Double
```

Thereafter, the *ReDim statement* can be used within the procedure to redefine the number of dimensions and elements in the array. The ReDim statement has the syntax

```
ReDim [Preserve] aname(sbs) [As type] [, aname(sbs) [As type]] . . .
```

where Preserve is an optional keyword used to preserve the data in an existing array when its size is changed, *aname* is the array name, *sbs* denotes the dimensions, and *type* is the data type of the variable. The following code gives an example of the use of the RecDim statement:

```
Option Explicit
Sub calc()
Dim a() As Double
ReDim a(3) As Double
a(0) = 5: a(1) = 8: a(2) = -6
ReDim a(5) As Double
MsgBox a(2)
End Sub
```

When this code is run, the first ReDim statement sets aside four memory locations (0 through 3) for the array. The second ReDim expands the upper limit to five and, in the process, wipes out the previous values. Hence, the message box would display a zero. If you want to retain the old values, the example can be modified by including the Preserve keyword, as in

```
Option Explicit
Sub calc()
Dim a() As Double
ReDim a(3) As Double
a(0) = 5: a(1) = 8: a(2) = -6
ReDim Preserve a(5) As Double
MsgBox a(2)
End Sub
```

In this case, the message box would display a "–6".

You can use the ReDim statement as many times as you desire within a procedure. However, you cannot declare an array of one data type and use ReDim later to change the array to another data type, unless the array is originally dimensioned as a Variant. In such cases, the type of the elements can be changed by using an As type clause, unless you're using the Preserve keyword, in which case no changes of data type are permitted.

If you use the Preserve keyword, you can resize only the last dimension of a multidimensional array, and you can't change the number of dimensions at all. For example, if your array has only one dimension, you can resize that dimension because it is the last and only dimension. However, if your array has two or more dimensions, you can change the size of only the last dimension and still preserve the contents of the array. For example, if you originally declare a three-dimensional array as

```
Dim velocity()
ReDim velocity(100, 20, 50)
```

you can increase the size of the last dimension with the statement

```
ReDim velocity(100, 20, 125)
```

If you make an array smaller than it was, data in the eliminated elements will be lost. If you pass an array to a procedure by reference, you can't redimension the array within the procedure.

13.2 RECORDS

Oftentimes you must deal with tables of data that contain different types of information. A classic example would be the periodic table:

	A	B	C	D
1	Periodic Table			
2				
3	Element	Symbol	Atomic Number	Atomic Weight
4	Actinium	Ac	89	227.0278
5	Aluminum	Al	13	26.98154
6	Americium	Am	95	243
7	Antimony	Sb	51	121.75
8	Argon	Ar	18	39.948
9	Arsenic	As	33	74.9216
10	Astatine	At	85	210
11	Barium	Ba	56	137.33
12	Berkelium	Bk	97	247

One way to handle such data would be to define an array for each column of information:

```
Dim Elname(118) As String
Dim Symbol(118) As String * 3
Dim AtomNumber(118) As Integer
Dim AtomicWeight(118) As Double
```

Although this would work, VBA provides an alternative, called a *record*, that allows you to store all the information in a single variable. To do that, you must first create a special variable type with the *Type statement*, the general form of which is

```
Type usertype
   itemname As type
   itemname As type
   itemname As type
     .
     .
     .
End Type
```

After establishing the type, you can dimension the record as

```
Dim varname(n) As usertype
```

Individual elements of the record are identified by appending a period and the type to the name, as in

```
varname(i).type
```

The following program shows how information from the periodic table could be stored in a record:

```
Option Explicit
Type ChemData
   Elname As String
   Symbol As String * 3
   AtomNumber As Integer
   AtomWeight As Double
End Type
Sub Periodic()
```

```
Dim Chem(118) As ChemData
Dim Msg As String
Chem(1).Elname = "Actinium"
Chem(1).Symbol = "Ac"
Chem(1).AtomNumber = 89
Chem(1).AtomWeight = 227.0278
    .
    .
    .

Msg = "Atomic number = " & Chem(1).AtomNumber
MsgBox Msg, , Chem(1).Elname
End Sub
```

When this Sub procedure is run, the following message box will be displayed:

The syntax for passing a record to a procedure is similar to that for an array, with one notable modification: the record's type must be specified in the procedure's argument list. For example, suppose that we wanted to pass `Chem()` to another procedure. Then the `Call` statement would be handled the same way as for an array:

```
Call Display(Chem())
```

However, the argument of the Sub statement must include the Type specification to inform the procedure that `Chem()` is a record.

```
Sub Display(Chem() As ChemData)
```

KEY TERMS

Average	Fixed-size array	ReDim statement
Bubble sort	Matrices	Timer function
Data structuring	Option Base statement	Type statement
Dynamic array	Record	Vectors

Problems

1. (*a*) Write Dim statements so that the following code will execute properly [note that the variable a holds real numbers (i.e., nonintegers)]:

```
Option Explicit
Sub calc()
Dim _____
n = 35000: x = "out of range": y = "in range"
Sheets("Sheet1").Select
Range("c1").Select
For i = 1 To n
  a(i) = ActiveCell.Value
  ActiveCell.Offset(1, 0).Select
```

```
Next i
sum = 0
For i = 1 To n
  sum = sum + a(i) ^ (i + 1)
Next i
If sum > 100 Then
  MsgBox x
Else
  MsgBox y
End If
Range("c1").Select
End Sub
```

(*b*) Suppose Sheet1 looked as follows:

	A	B	C
1			10
2			
3			
4			
5			
6			
7			
8			
9			
10			

What would happen when `Sub calc()` was executed?

2. If the following code is implemented, fill in the values that follow:

```
Option Explicit
Sub Test()
Dim i As Integer, j As Integer, n As Integer
Dim a(10, 10) As Double
n = 4
For i = 1 To n
  For j = 1 To n
    a(i, j) = 2 * (i * j)
  Next j
Next i
End Sub
a(1, 1) =    _____
a(2, 3) =    _____
a(5, 5) =    _____
```

3. Fill in the values of the variables at each point indicated in the following algorithm:

```
Option Explicit
Sub Calc()
Dim m as integer, n As Integer, i As Integer
Dim a(100) As Double, x(100) As Double
m = 1
a(0) = -1
```

```
                                a(0)  a(1)    x(0)      x(1)     m       n
                              _____ _____   _____     _____   _____   _____
Call Switch(a(), m)
a(1) = a(m)
                              _____ _____   _____     _____   _____   _____
End Sub
Sub Switch(x, n)
Dim m as integer, i As Integer
Dim a(10) As Double
                              _____ _____   _____     _____   _____   _____
m = n - 2
x(1) = 2
x(2) = 7
a(1) = -5
n = m + 3
                              _____ _____   _____     _____   _____   _____
End Sub
```

4. Modify the code from Hands-on Exercise 13.1 so that it converts the temperatures from Celsius to Fahrenheit and displays the results in column C.

5. Write VBA code to implement the following formula that determines the average and standard deviation of the values in an array:

$$\bar{y} = \frac{\displaystyle\sum_{i=1}^{n} y_i}{n}$$

$$s_y = \sqrt{\frac{\displaystyle\sum_{i=1}^{n}\left(y_i^2\right) - \frac{\left(\displaystyle\sum_{i=1}^{n} y_i\right)^2}{n}}{n-1}}$$

Note that the values are real. Enter the numbers in column A of a sheet labeled *Average,* starting at A4. Design the main program so that it detects whether the user leaves cells A4:A5 blank. If so, display a message box alerting the user that the average and standard deviation require at least two values, and terminate the program with cell A3 selected.

6. Write a well-structured VBA Sub procedure that utilizes the bubble sort to sort an array (*a*) in descending order and (*b*) in either ascending or descending order, depending on the value of an argument passed to the procedure.

7. Write a well-structured VBA Sub procedure that utilizes the bubble sort to sort several arrays of values in ascending order, depending the values in one of the columns. Use the following data:

Substance	State	Density (kg/m3)	Thermal conductivity (W/(m K)	Specific heat (J/(kg K)
Air	Gas	1.186	0.0259	1005
Asphalt	Solid	2115	0.062	920
Carbon dioxide	Gas	1.789	0.0166	852

Iron	Solid	7870	80.2	447
Mercury	Liquid	13,562	8.9	139
Water	Liquid	997	0.0186	4180

Test your code by sorting the data by state and by specific heat.

8. Write a well-structured VBA Sub procedure that utilizes the bubble sort to sort a record according to one of its values. Test the code with the data from Problem 7.

9. Use the bubble sort program from Hands-on Exercise 13.2 to verify that its execution time is proportional to the square of the number being sorted. Do this by sorting arrays of length n = 256, 512, 1024, 2048, 4096, and 8192. Use Excel to make a plot of log time versus log n. Then, fit a power model to the plot with the Trend Line feature of Excel. Interpret your results.

10. Develop a program that takes a matrix of data and converts it into a vector.

11. A modification of the *ideal-gas law*, that can handle nonideal conditions is the *Redlich-Kwong* equation of state,

$$p = \frac{RT}{(v-b)} - \frac{a}{v(v+b)\sqrt{T}}$$

where

$$a = 0.427 \frac{R^2 T_c^{2.5}}{p_c} \qquad b = 0.0866 R \frac{T_c}{p_c}$$

where p is the pressure of the gas (atm), V is the volume (L), R is the universal gas constant (= 0.08205 (atm L)/(mole K)), T is temperature [K], P_c is the critical pressure of the substance (atm), and T_c = the critical temperature of the substance [K]. The values of T_c and P_c for these parameters have been complied for numerous gases. The following table shows four of them:

Compound	T_c	P_c
Methane	190.6	45.4
Ethylene	282.4	49.7
Nitrogen	126.2	33.5
Water (vapor)	647.1	217.6

Develop a program to compute pressure for each of these gases for a particular temperature and volume. Test it for T = 400 K and V = 100 L. Us a record to store the critical temperatures and pressures.

14

Creating and Accessing Files

Up to now, we have input data into our VBA programs from a spreadsheet by selecting a cell and assigning its value to a variable, as in the following code:

```
Range("a1").Select
x = ActiveCell.Value
```

Alternatively, we have output data in a similar fashion:

```
Range("a1").Select
ActiveCell.Value = x
```

In addition, we can use message and input boxes to enter single values, as well as output messages and information, as in the following code:

```
Msgbox "The answer is " & x
```

Although all of these approaches are quite useful for problems involving small quantities of data, they can be limiting when you have to deal with large quantities of data. Further, there will be many occasions upon which you and your colleagues will receive data files over the Internet or via "snail mail." In such cases, you must become familiar with accessing and creating such files.

SECTIONS

- 14.1 Sequential Files
- 14.2 Other File Operations

OBJECTIVES

After reading this chapter, you should be able to

- Create a file from within a VBA procedure.
- Read data from a file into a VBA procedure.
- Create a file with Excel that can be read by VBA.
- Allow the user to browse for a file name for both accessing and saving files.

14.1   SEQUENTIAL FILES

Two fundamental actions are required to incorporate files into your macros:

- Writing data from your program into a file.
- Inputting data from a file back into your program.

The following simple example illustrates how to write data to a file, the key statements are highlighted:

```
Option Explicit
Sub OutputToFile()
Dim a As Double, b As Double, StudentName As String
a = 5
b = 6
StudentName = "Ima Engineer"
Open "a:\test.dat" For Output As #1
Write #1, a, b, StudentName
Close #1
End Sub
```

After constants are assigned to the variables a, b, and StudentName, an *Open statement* is needed to create the file. Besides opening the file, this statement serves three other purposes:

- It specifies the name of the file that is to be created: *"a:\test.dat"*. This is the name by which the file is referenced outside your program—that is, on your hard drive or a diskette. The complete path to the location of the file must be specified as a string. Notice that this example is set up to create the file on a diskette in drive a.
- It specifies that data will be *output* from your program into the file in question.
- It assigns a number to the file: *#1*. This is the number by which the file is referenced within your program.

Then a *Write statement* is used to actually write the information into the file. Finally, a *Close statement* is used to close the file. Notice how, in both cases, the file number (#1) is used to let VBA know which file you are manipulating. This might not seem too important here, since we have only one file open, but in other cases you might have several files open simultaneously.

After the program is executed, a file named *test.dat* containing the numbers 5 and 6 and the string constant "Ima Engineer" will reside on your diskette. To verify this, go to a word processor or text editor, and open the file a:\test.dat. You should see something like this:

Notice that commas are used to *delimit* (i.e., separate) the values.

Now suppose that you want to reverse the process and input the data from the file into another program. Here's a simple example of how this would be done:

```
Option Explicit
Sub InputFromFile()
Dim a As Double, b As Double, StudentName As String
Open "a:\test.dat" For Input As #2
Input #2, a, b, StudentName
Close #2
MsgBox a & " " & b & " " & StudentName
End Sub
```

Notice the differences from the other example:

- The Open statement differs in that now we specify that data will be *input* from the file into the program.
- We've used a new number to reference the file within your program (#2). Since this is a completely different program, we actually could have used #1, but we wanted to illustrate the fact that the file number is your choice (as long as it is in the range from 1 to 511).
- We use an Input # statement to input the values from the file into the program.

After this program is executed, the following message box corroborates that the values are now resident in the variables a, b, and StudentName within your program:

To summarize, a file is opened with the Open statement,

```
Open pathname For mode As [#]filenumber
```

where `pathname` is a string expression that specifies a file name (pathname should include the complete path to the file), `mode` is a keyword specifying the file mode (Append, Binary, Input, Output, or Random; if the mode is not specified, the file is opened for Random access), and `filenumber` is a valid file number in the range from 1 to 511.

Once the file is opened, its data can be accessed by a Write # statement,

```
Write #filenumber, [outputlist]
```

where `outputlist` is one or more comma-delimited numeric or string expressions to write to a file.

Alternatively, the data can be retrieved by an Input # statement,

```
Input #filenumber, varlist
```

where `varlist` is a comma-delimited list of variables that are assigned values read from the file. Note that `varlist` cannot be an array; however, variables that describe an element of an array or a user-defined type may be used.

Finally, the file is closed with

```
Close #filenumber
```

A question remains: Suppose that you are using a loop to input an array from a file. If you don't know the number of values in the array, how do you know when to terminate the loop? The solution is provided by a function called *EOF* (an acronym for *End Of File*). Its general syntax is

```
EOF (filenumber)
```

This function returns an Integer containing the Boolean value True (1) when the end of a file has been reached. As long as the end of the file has not been reached, the EOF function returns False (0). Here is an example of how it is used:

```
nd = -1
Do
  If EOF(1) Then Exit Do
  nd = nd + 1
  Input #1, Temp(nd), Dens(nd)
Loop
Close #1
```

In this case, we want to read two parallel arrays (i.e., two columns of data) that start with a subscript of 0. A counter (nd) is first set equal to –1. Then we enter a Do/If/Exit loop. Since we have just started reading the file, we are obviously not at the end of the loop, so EOF(1) would reflect that fact by returning False. Consequently, the loop would not be exited. The counter would be incremented to 0, and the two variables would be input into the arrays, using nd as the subscript. The process would continue until the end of the file was reached. At that point, EOF(1) would return True, the loop would terminate, and nd would be equal to the number of values.

14.1.1 Hands-on Exercise: File Manipulations

This exercise runs you through the following file manipulations:

- Using Excel to create a data file
- Reading the file you created back into Excel, using VBA
- Creating a file with a VBA code
- Importing the VBA file back into Excel

As an engineer, you will become accustomed to dealing with large quantities of data. The purpose of the exercise you will carry out here is to acquaint you with some simple approaches to inputting and outputting data from files.

STEP 1: Start up Excel, and enter the following data for the temperature and density of water into your worksheet:

```
A1: 0      B1: 0.99987
A2: 4      B2: 1.00000
A3: 8      B3: 0.99988
A4: 12     B4: 0.99952
A5: 16     B5: 0.99897
A6: 20     B6: 0.99823
A7: 24     B7: 0.99733
A8: 28     B8: 0.99626
```

Save the file with these data on your diskette drive (usually a:\) as a comma-delimited file, *TempDensH2O.csv*. To do this, select **File, Save As.** Type in the name TempDensH2O, and then select the comma-delimited option (.csv) from the *Save as type* pull-down menu:

File name:	TempDensH2O	▼	Save
Save as type:	CSV (Comma delimited)	▼	Cancel

```
Microsoft Excel 5.0/95 Workbook
Microsoft Excel 97-2002 & 5.0/95 Workbook
CSV (Comma delimited)
Microsoft Excel 4.0 Worksheet
Microsoft Excel 3.0 Worksheet
Microsoft Excel 2.1 Worksheet
```

When you do this, you should be prompted with a message which warns you that you'll be saving only the active sheet. Since that is precisely what you want to do, hit **OK**. Then close the file. At this point, you might get an additional message to which you would respond "No," since you want to save the file in the existing format (i.e., comma delimited).

STEP 2: Next, open a new workbook, and immediately save it on a:\ as a normal Excel file: TempDensH2O.xls. Go into VBA, insert a module, and type in the following program, line by line, all the while observing my comments:

```
Option Explicit
Sub Calc()
Dim i As Integer, nd As Integer
Dim Temp(1000) As Double, Dens(1000) As Double
```

The next executable line opens the file for input (i.e., input to your program from the file):

```
'fetch data from the file
Open "a:\TempDensH2O.csv" For Input As #1
```

STEP 3: Include a Do/If/Exit loop that (a) reads in the data until it gets to the end of the file [and EOF(1) tests true] and (b) counts the data (using the variable nd):

```
nd = -1
Do
  If EOF(1) Then Exit Do
  nd = nd + 1
  Input #1, Temp(nd), Dens(nd)
Loop
Close #1
```

STEP 4: Finally, to check that everything has worked properly, we can display the values back on the worksheet, using standard commands:

```
'Display values on the worksheet
Sheets("Sheet1").Select
Range("a1").Select
For i = 0 To nd
  ActiveCell.Value = Temp(i)
```

```
  ActiveCell.Offset(0, 1).Select
  ActiveCell.Value = Dens(i)
  ActiveCell.Offset(1, -1).Select
Next i
Range("a1").Select
```

STEP 5: Set up a button to run this Sub procedure and execute the code. The final result should look like this:

	A	B	C	D	E
1	0	0.99987			
2	4	1		RUN	
3	8	0.99988			
4	12	0.99952			
5	16	0.99897			
6	20	0.99823			
7	24	0.99733			
8	28	0.99626			
9					

STEP 6: Next, let's modify the data by applying some simple conversions. We'll convert the temperature to Kelvin by $T(K) = T(^{\circ}C) + 273.15$, and we'll convert the density to kg/m^3 by multiplying by 1000:

```
'apply conversions
For i = 0 To nd
  Temp(i) = Temp(i) + 273.15
  Dens(i) = Dens(i) * 1000
Next i
```

STEP 7: The next executable line opens the file for output (i.e., output from your program to the file). Notice that we use a different file name:

```
'create a file
Open "a:\DeConv.csv" For Output As #2
```

STEP 8: We include a For/Next loop that writes the data to the file:

```
For i = 0 To nd
  Write #2, Temp(i), Dens(i)
Next i
Close #2
```

The final, complete code should look like this:

```
Option Explicit
Sub Calc()
Dim i As Integer, nd As Integer
Dim Temp(1000) As Double, Dens(1000) As Double
'fetch data from the file
Open "a:\TempDensH2O.csv" For Input As #1
nd = -1
Do
```

```
      If EOF(1) Then Exit Do
      nd = nd + 1
      Input #1, Temp(nd), Dens(nd)
Loop
Close #1
'display values on the worksheet
Sheets("Sheet1").Select
Range("a1").Select
For i = 0 To nd
   ActiveCell.Value = Temp(i)
   ActiveCell.Offset(0, 1).Select
   ActiveCell.Value = Dens(i)
   ActiveCell.Offset(1, -1).Select
Next i
Range("a1").Select
'apply conversions
For i = 0 To nd
   Temp(i) = Temp(i) + 273.15
   Dens(i) = Dens(i) * 1000
Next i
'create a file
Open "a:\DeConv.csv" For Output As #2
For i = 0 To nd
   Write #2, Temp(i), Dens(i)
Next i
Close #2
End Sub
```

Run the program, and it should create a new file, DeConv.csv, back on a:\.

STEP 9: Now return to Excel to open the file DeConvXX.csv. If all has worked properly, the converted temperatures and densities should be showing on the screen:

	A	B	C
1	273.15	999.87	
2	277.15	1000	
3	281.15	999.88	
4	285.15	999.52	
5	289.15	998.97	
6	293.15	998.23	
7	297.15	997.33	
8	301.15	996.26	
9			

14.2 OTHER FILE OPERATIONS

VBA allows you to access Excel's built-in dialogue boxes. The next two methods are very handy for opening and saving files.

14.2.1 GetOpenFilename Method

If you needed to get a file name from a user, you could certainly write an input box for the purpose. This is not the best solution, however, because most users have a difficult time recalling the exact file name, let alone its complete path. VBA provides a superior alternative that allows you to display Excel's *Open Dialogue Box*. This is the familiar box that Excel displays when you make the menu selection: **File, Open**. The syntax for the method is

```
Application.GetOpenFilename([FFilt],[FIndex], _
                           [Title],[BText],[MultSel])
```

where

FFilt =   A string specifying the file-filtering criteria. The string consists of pairs of file filter strings, followed by the MS-DOS wild-card file filter specification, with each part and each pair separated by commas. For example, the following string specifies two file filters—text and comma-separated files:

```
"Text Files (*.txt),*.txt,Word Documents (*.doc),*.doc"
```

If omitted, this argument defaults to "All Files (*.*),*.*".

FIndex =   The index numbers of the default file-filtering criteria, from 1 to the number of filters specified in *FFilt*. If this argument is omitted or is greater than the number of filters present, the first file filter is used.

Title =   The title of the dialog box. If this argument is omitted, the title is "Open."

BTxt =   Ignore (Macintosh only).

MultSel =   Set to True to allow multiple file names to be selected. Set to False to allow only one file name to be selected. The default value is False.

Although the GetOpenFilename method displays the Open Dialogue Box, it doesn't open the file. Rather, it returns the files name and path selected by the user. Then you can use this information to do whatever you desire with the file name.

Here's an example of how GetOpenFilename is used: Suppose that you want the user to choose a text file with the extension *.txt, *.prn, or *.csv, with the default being *.txt. The following code will do the job:

```
Option Explicit
Sub Test()
Dim FileName As String
Call GetName(FileName)
If FileName = "False" Then
  MsgBox "You didn't select a file name"
Else
  MsgBox "You selected the file: " & FileName
End If
End Sub
Sub GetName(FileName)
Dim FFilt As String
FFilt = "Text Files (*.txt),*.txt," & _
        "Space Delimited Files (*.prn),*.prn," & _
        "Comma Delimited Files (*.csv),*.csv,"
FileName = Application.GetOpenFilename(FFilt, 1, "Choose a _
                                       File")

End Sub
```

The Sub procedure GetName implements the GetOpenFileName method. Notice that, because the *FFilt* is fairly verbose, we store it first in a string variable. When the method is executed, the following dialogue box is displayed:

The user then selects a file name and clicks the Open button. When this is done, the file name and path are returned to the Sub, where it can be assigned to a variable. In our example, the file name is then returned to the calling Sub. There, the name is displayed, or an error message is displayed if the user did not select a file. For example, if the user selected the file 1999Data.txt, the following message box would be displayed:

If a file was not selected (that is, if the user clicked the Cancel button), the GetOpen-Filename method returns "False".

In a larger application, you would use the name to perform some action, such as opening the file with a statement like

```
Open FileName For Input As #1
```

14.2.2 GetSaveAsFilename Method

The *GetSaveAsFilename* method operates the same way as the GetOpenFilename method, but it displays the familiar Excel *Save As* dialogue box. The syntax of the statement is

```
Application.GetSaveAsFilename([InitName],[FFilt], _
                        {FIndex],[Title])
```

where `InitName` is a string specifying a suggested file name. If this argument is omitted, Excel uses the name of the active workbook. All the optional arguments are as in the *GetOpenFilename* method.

KEYTERMS

Close statement	GetSaveAsFilename	Output statement
Delimit	Input statement	Save As type
End of File (EOF)	Open Dialogue box	Write statement
GetOpenFilename	Open statement	

Problems

1. Set up a column of 20 random numbers starting at A1. Convert these numbers into values by selecting them and then making the menus selections: **Edit, Copy** and **Edit, Paste Special, Values**. Save this data as a comma-delimited file called Random.csv. Write a VBA program that accomplishes the following:

    *   Uses the GetOpenFilename method to allow the user to select the file name and path.
    *   Reads the numbers into an array
    *   Sorts the array in ascending order using the bubble sort (flowchart is shown below).
    *   Writes the sorted array to another worksheet and to a data file called Random.out

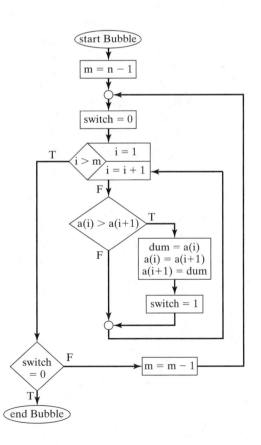

2. Create a macro that reads the following table of data from a worksheet:

	A	B	C	D
1	Physical properties of common gases at 1 atm and 20°C			
2				
3	Gas	Molecular weight	Density (kg/m3)	Viscosity (N s/m2)
4	Air	28.96	1.205	18.00
5	Carbon dioxide	44.01	1.840	14.80
6	Carbon monoxide	28.01	1.160	18.20
7	Helium	4.003	0.166	19.70
8	Hydrogen	2.016	0.084	9.05
9	Methane	16.04	0.668	13.40
10	Nitrogen	28.02	1.160	17.60
11	Nitrogen dioxide	44.02	1.825	14.50
12	Nitric oxide	30.01	1.233	19.00
13	Oxygen	32	1.330	20.00
14	Water	18.02	0.747	10.20

Have the macro write these data to a file.

15

Custom Dialogue Boxes

Message and input boxes are extremely useful vehicles for communicating with users. However, they are limited in that they can only deal with a few values at a time.

In the present chapter, I will describe a more powerful tool that permits much more flexibility. Called *custom dialogue boxes* (or *user forms*), these allow you to design your own boxes to both obtain and display information. In contrast to message and input boxes, they can include numerous buttons, messages, input slots, etc. In addition, they can include other user input tools such as radio buttons, spin buttons, scroll bars, etc. Hence, they provide a way to develop fairly sophisticated user interfaces.

OBJECTIVES

After reading this chapter, you should be able to

- Create your own custom dialogue box to obtain information and display results.
- Use an event handler to automatically display a custom dialogue box.
- Use custom dialogue boxes as an input vehicle for large projects.

15.1   A SIMPLE CUSTOM DIALOGUE BOX

As with so many other parts of this book, the best way to introduce you to custom dialogue boxes is with a hands-on exercise. So turn on your computer and fire up Excel.

15.1.1   Hands-on Exercise: Developing a Simple Custom Dialogue Box

Let's develop a custom dialogue box that adds two numbers together and displays the result. As always, we employ a simple example so that you can learn the basic concepts without having to deal with complicating details.

STEP 1: Open a new workbook and save it as *SimpUserForm.xls*. Switch over to the VBE, and make certain that the correct VBA project (VBA Project SimpUser-Form.xls) is selected in the Project Explorer Window. Insert a user form with the following menu selection:

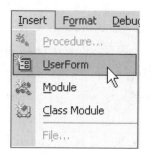

A blank User form, along with a Toolbox palette, will be displayed:

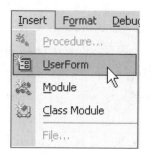

Notice that the Properties Window now contains a series of entries that define the properties of the user form:

STEP 2: We will now customize the user form by changing some of these entries. First, select the Caption entry with the mouse, and change the caption field to "Simple Addition Wizard":

Notice that, as you type, the user form's caption is changed:

Return to the Properties Window, and change the (Name) field to "SimpleAddition".[1] This renames the object that is the user form. The Properties Window should now look like the following:

---

[1] In contrast to captions, no spaces are allowed for (Name) fields.

STEP 3: Next, we will create some labels and text boxes to allow the user to enter the values to be added and to display the results. Go to Toolbox palette and click on the Label tool (if the Toolbox palette ever disappears, you can always invoke the menu commands **View, Toolbox** to make it reappear):

Click on the Label tool, **A**, move the mouse to the user form, and drag out a label rectangle like the following:

Notice that when this label object is selected, the Properties Window displays the properties of the label, not those of the user form. Click on the Caption property, and change the caption field to First Number. Then, click on the Font property and the button to the right of that field, [...], and set the font to Arial, the size to 11, and the font style to bold:

Next, click OK. You may need to resize the label box to look like this:

Now, click on the Text Box button in the Toolbox palette:

Back on the user form, drag out a text box to the right of the label. The result should look like this:

With the text box selected, change the Name field in the Properties Window to "InputFirst":

STEP 4: Now we would like to create

- A second label and text box for the second number to be added and
- A third label and text box for the total.

To accomplish these tasks, you could obviously just repeat the actions described in Step 3. However, let's explore another alternative.

We went through a little bit of trouble to get the first number's label and text box to look just right. It would be nice to create the other label and text boxes in a simpler fashion. We can do that by copying and pasting.

Go to the user form and select the first number label. Then hold down the Ctrl and Shift keys, and select the text box. Thus, both the label and the box will be selected:

Next, select **Edit, Copy** from the menu (or hit the hot-key combination *Ctrl–c*) to copy the selection to the clipboard. Then, paste the selection back on the user form. (Select **Edit, Paste** from the menu, or hit *Ctrl–v*.) Move the new label and text box so that they are positioned properly below the original ones. Select the new label and change its Caption property to "Second number". Select the new text box and change its (Name) to "InputSecond".

Repeat these actions to create a third label, with Caption field "Total", and a text box, with (Name) field "OutputTotal". The final result should look like this:

STEP 5: Now we need to place some buttons that will allow us to make things happen. Use the CommandButton tool and place the buttons as shown:

Select the left button and change its (Name) and Caption fields to "Add". Select the right button and change its (Name) and Caption fields to "Quit". For both buttons, click on the Font property and set the font to Arial, the size to 11, and the font style to bold. Also, make the Add button the default button by changing its Default property to True. This is done so that the Add button will be preselected. Thus, the user merely has to hit the return key to perform the addition. In contrast, the Quit button must be explicitly selected to terminate the program. The resulting dialogue box should look like this:

STEP 6: Now we need to write the VBA code that executes when the Add and Quit buttons are clicked. Start by double-clicking the Add button. A code window should open up with the following information:

```
Option Explicit
Private Sub Add_Click()
End Sub
```

Enter the following block of code between the Private Sub and End Sub statements:

```
Dim First As Double, Second As Double, Total As Double
'Get the values to be added
First = InputFirst.Value
Second = InputSecond.Value
'Perform the addition
Total = First + Second
'Display the summation
OutputTotal.Value = Total
```

Select **View, Object** (or hit the Shift–F7 shortcut) to get back to the user form, and then double-click on the Quit button. Another Private Sub and End Sub statement should be added for that button:

```
Private Sub Quit_Click()
End Sub
```

Enter the statement

```
Unload SimpleAddition
```

in this Sub.

STEP 7: To test your program, select **Insert, Module**, and enter the following short Sub:

```
Option Explicit
Sub Adder()
SimpleAddition.Show
End Sub
```

When you run this Sub procedure, the user form should appear and you can test your program. For example, you might have

The user can run the program over and over by changing the numbers and striking the Add button. When finished, the user can click the Quit button to terminate the program.

STEP 8: Finally, you can add an *event handler* that will automatically bring up your user form when the workbook is opened. In the VBE, double-click on the *This-Workbook* item in the Project Explorer. Change the left field at the top of the code window to Workbook. (Use the drop-down list.) You should now see

```
Workbook                          Open

Option Explicit

Private Sub Workbook_Open()

End Sub
```

The automatically created Workbook_Open Sub allows you to enter code that will be executed when the workbook is opened. Enter the one statement that will display the user form, as shown in the following code:

```
Option Explicit
Private Sub Workbook_Open()
SimpleAddition.Show
End Sub
```

Save your workbook and close it out. Reopen your workbook, and the user form should appear.

15.2   CUSTOM DIALOGUE BOXES AND MODULES

The foregoing example was implemented entirely within the Sub procedure that was triggered by clicking the Add button. Although this approach is fine for simple calculations, most engineering-oriented applications usually involve more complicated computations that use several Sub and Function procedures. Therefore, we will now explore how custom dialogue boxes are integrated with larger programs.

15.2.1 Hands-on Exercise: Custom Dialogue Box and Modules

Let's develop a program to compute the velocity of a free-falling parachutist, using the formula

$$v(t) = v_0 e^{-(c_d/m)t} + \frac{gm}{c_d}\left(1 - e^{-(c_d/m)t}\right) \qquad (15\text{-}1)$$

where $v(t)$ is the parachutist's downward velocity [m/s]; v_0 is the parachutist's initial downward velocity; t is time [s]; g is the acceleration due to gravity [$\cong 9.8$ m/s^2]; m is the jumper's mass [kg]; and c_d is a proportionality constant, called the drag coefficient [kg/s], that parameterizes air resistance.

STEP 1: Open a new workbook, save it as *ParaForm.xls*, and switch over to the VBE. Using the same approach as in Section 15.1.1, develop a user form named *ParameterInput*, as in Figure 15.1.

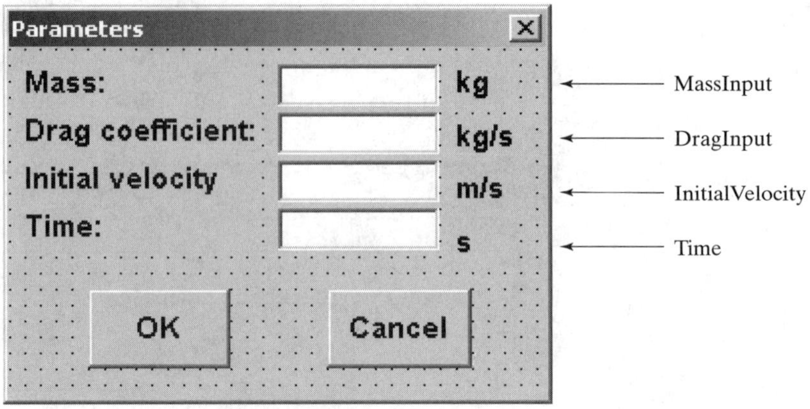

Figure 15.1. User form to input the parameters for the falling-parachutist problem. The arrows at the right indicate the names of the text boxes into which the parameters are entered.

STEP 2: Insert a new module, and type in the following code:

```
Option Explicit
Public m As Double, cd As Double, t As Double, vi As Double
Sub Parameters()
Dim v As Double
Const g As Double = 9.81
'Input parameters
ParameterInput.Show
'Calculate velocity
v = vi * Exp(-cd / m * t) + g * m / cd * (1 - Exp(-cd / m * t))
'Display results
MsgBox "The velocity = " & v & "m/s"
End Sub
```

When this code is run, the form will be displayed by the statement

```
ParameterInput.Show
```

The Public statement is included so that this Sub will have access to the parameter values entered on the user form.

STEP 3: Enter the following code for the Cancel and OK buttons:

```
Option Explicit
Private Sub Cancel_Click()
Unload ParameterInput
End
End Sub
Private Sub OK_Click()
m = MassInput.Value
cd = DragInput.Value
vi = InitialVelocity.Value
t = InitialTime.Value
Unload ParameterInput
End Sub
```

Notice that the Cancel button merely unloads the form and ends the macro. The OK button takes the values entered on the user form, assigns them to Public variables, and then unloads the form.

STEP 4: Go back to Excel, and create a button to run the Sub procedure *Parameters*. When you click on this button, the statement `ParameterInput.Show` will display the user form. Enter the following values:

If you click OK, this result should appear:

KEY TERMS

Ctrl-c	Frames	Text box
Ctrl-v	Label tool	Toolbox palette
Custom dialogue box	Parameters	User forms
Event handler	Properties window	

Problems

1. The program

```
Option Explicit
Sub Test()
Dim UsersName As String
UsersName = InputBox("Please enter your name", "Name Input")
End Sub
```

will display the following Input Box:

Employ a user form to develop your own "homemade" Input Box. Use a message box to display the name that was entered to verify that your program works properly.

2. The following equation predicts the velocity of a falling object:

$$v(t) = v_0 e^{-\frac{c_d}{m}t} + \frac{gm}{c_d}\left(1 - e^{-\frac{c_d}{m}t}\right)$$

Develop a VBA macro and user form to

*   Input values of m, c_d, v_0, and t.
*   Compute $v(t)$.
*   Display the result.

Use message boxes to display error messages when the user enters erroneous inputs (e.g., a mass or drag less than or equal to 0).

3. Develop a VBA macro to make temperature conversions. Display the converted temperature as a message box. Employ the following user form to input the desired values:

Note that the borders labeled "Input Units" and "Output Units" are referred to as *frames*. They can be created with the Frame tool:

References

Chapra, S.C. and Canale, R.P. 1994. Introduction to Computing for Engineers, 2nd Ed., McGraw-Hill, New York, N.Y.

Chapra, S.C. and Canale, R.P. 2001. Numerical Methods for Engineers, 4th Ed., McGraw-Hill, New York, N.Y.

Walkenbach, J. 1999. Excel 2000 for Windows for Dummies, IDG Books, Foster City, CA..

Walkenbach, J. 1999. Microsoft Excel 2000 Power Programming With VBA, IDG Books, Foster City, CA.

Index